There's a *Woman* in Here!

The trials, tribulations and triumphs
of the first female psychologist to work behind the walls
of Jackson Prison, as revealed in her journals

Jean Becker Walsh

Cover painting by Jean Becker Walsh

Cover designed by Nate Swartzlander,
Legacy Printing – Jackson, MI

Library of Congress Control Number: 2013946547

Cataloging-in-Publication data

Walsh, Jean Becker.
    There's a woman in here! : the trials, tribulations and triumphs of the first
female psychologist to work behind the walls of Jackson Prison, as revealed in her
journals / Jean Becker Walsh.
        p. cm.
        ISBN-13: 978-1491250471
        ISBN-10: 149125047X

1.Walsh, Jean Becker. 2. Prison psychologists --Michigan --Biography. 3. Prison
psychology. 4. Prisoners --Mental health services --United States. 5. Michigan --
State Prison, Jackson. 6. Prisoners --Michigan --Jackson. 7. Prisons --United
States. 8. Corrections --United States. I. Title.

HV6089 .W35 2013
365/.66 --dc23   2013946547

There's a *Woman* in Here!

Dedication

This book is dedicated to Dr. Ernest A. Smith
whose words changed my life

Table of Contents

Figures

Thoughts on Prison
By the Author

Prison is a terrible place. Each number represents some form of human tragedy, for victim and perpetrator of the crime alike. Society has set forth the rules which must be obeyed; the men behind bars are those who bear the stigma of having failed to live up to societal expectations. It is decreed that they be kept apart from the rest of us while an attempt is made to "rehabilitate" before we must encounter them again in the streets. We are afraid of them, of these non-conformists who cannot or will not abide by our rules. And we also want them punished. Somehow it fulfills our belief in an ordered universe, one in which justice prevails (although we continue to pay lip service to mercy, as well.)

I can remember my first glimpse of a prison, from the safety of our family car. I was too small to understand fully, but the lowered voices of my parents as they pointed it out, with the starkness of its dark walls and barred windows, conveyed their attitudes to me. Fear of what might be unleashed, should those walls suddenly fall down, was surely there, but mixed with it, a great curiosity. What sort of monsters were these who must be kept apart, in cages like animals? As I peered through the glass with big eyes, I never dreamed that one day I would spend years behind such walls, working with and coming to know many of these men we label misfits, and sometimes, "dangerous to society."

The work that I did inside Jackson Prison ended many years ago. I had found it to be draining emotionally, routinely frustrating--- but yes, sometimes tremendously rewarding as well. But I left for the last time in 1981 when the barred steel doors closed behind me. My access to that other world ended when I turned in my keys and ID pass. I left it to others to continue my work and inhabit my office. I am sure they also learned, as I had, the frustrations of becoming a part of that strange social order behind the walls. I returned to live in the world of normalcy and turned my back on the prison. Yet to this day I find it still confronts me. My experiences there, where the bizarre is commonplace and where sanity and insanity intermingle, satisfied the curiosity of my childhood. The horror that I discovered inside and that still haunts me, is not that the cages contain monsters, for I found that prisoners are indeed only men. It is that ordinary men are sometimes capable of committing monstrous, unspeakable acts. That knowledge remains with me in ghostly images, even as I attempt to share with readers my day to day activities, after a commitment to becoming an influence for good led me to work behind the walls of Jackson Prison.

Foreword

The Michigan Department of Corrections' historic decision to employ female staff in prisons housing only male inmates came about as a natural progression in the state's evolving effort to ensure equality in employee hiring practices. While there was general consensus among department administrators that "the time was right," and ethically, it was the "right thing to do," actual implementation of the idea was fraught with difficulties.

The facility selected for initiating the precedent-setting practice was the Reception and Guidance Center, which was located within the State Prison of Southern Michigan, and which, at that time, served as the initial processing facility for all male prisoners sentenced to serve state supervised prison time.

Figure 1 - Aerial View of State Prison of Southern Michigan (Jackson Prison)

Since the makeup of the unit's prisoner population routinely included physically dangerous and sexually predatory individuals, the plan to employ female staff raised serious concern about whether adequate custodial procedures could be developed that would adequately insure a female employee's safety.

13

While the unit's top administrators possessed a high degree of confidence in the professional competence of its custodial staff, some employees thought the task too risky and resented the additional custodial burden. Moreover, the Department of Corrections' mandate to hire females left little time to develop an appropriate model for managing the protection of women functioning in a male prisoner setting. Thus, when the first woman entered the unit's cell block, both she and male staff faced an "on the job" training challenge.

Of additional concern was the viability of expecting young, isolated, testosterone-driven male prisoners to accommodate a female presence without exhibiting dangerous or predatory overreaction.

As the Reception and Guidance Center's program manager and head of its Psychological Services Unit, I assumed a personal role in carrying out the mandate to hire women. The plan was to eventually employ both female psychologists and female counselors. We decided the most pressing need was to fill an entry level psychologist position. We advertised, and Eugenia Becker (Jean) proved to be the outstanding applicant. She was promptly brought on board, and the precedent-setting venture began.

Of course, any woman willing to face the implacable pioneering challenges for the sake of a professional career must be made of "the right stuff." She must, of necessity, possess inordinate strength and courage as well as an enduring desire for professional humanitarian service. It was the Department of Correction's good fortune that Jean Becker proved to be such a woman. As the head of PSU, it was my privilege to manage overall supervision of Jean's training as a "new psychologist recruit." I monitored her progress through personal observation, reviewing her reports, and by soliciting regular feedback from other PSU and custodial staff. I was gratified to see her professional wings sprout and grow. I could not help but empathize as she struggled to forge a professional image while working in what was sometimes a hostile environment. I saw moments when she appeared frustrated and angry, but also saw her determination and indomitable spirit, as she battled the idiosyncrasies inherent in a male prison environment, and though it was that very anger and frustration that led Jean to eventually resign her post, the trail she blazed still serves as an enduring inspiration for women who seek to serve in any part of the male criminal justice system. I was sorry when Jean left the Reception and Guidance Center, but could well understand her motivation. This book is her intriguing account of what must have seemed at the time to be a nightmarish emotional and physical challenge to professional success, but by enduring, the implacable Jean Becker Walsh bravely forged a new career path for herself and the cadre of women that followed.

Now on a personal note, Jean's professional development as a clinician proved a valuable asset to the Psychological Services Unit, and helped to prove the Department of Corrections' experiment with women working in men's prisons ultimately a long-term success. Moreover, and to my delight, I discovered Jean possesses qualities of warmth, caring, sensitivity and loyalty that quickly invite closeness and enduring friendship. She has the heart and soul of an artist and I am privileged to count Jean as a lifelong friend.

Donald Houseworth, Ph.D.
Regional Administrator, Retired
Michigan Department of Corrections

Acknowledgments

First, I would like to thank whoever it was in the Michigan Department of Corrections that made the decision in 1975 to begin the experiment of having women work with male inmates in a maximum security prison! When that decision was implemented, it fell to three interviewers from the Reception and Guidance Center to decide whether they should take a chance on hiring me as the person to fill such a position, which would mean my working as a psychologist, evaluating and providing therapy to inmates at the State Prison of Southern Michigan. When I accepted the position and they became my supervisors there, they gave me time to rise above the early unease I felt, in what was to me, a completely foreign and frightening setting. Dr. Don Houseworth, who has written the foreword for this book, was one of those interviewers and then my supervisor, and I am so pleased that our friendship, which began in Seven Block, has endured through all the years since that time.

As I took on my duties in Seven Block (Reception and Guidance Center), I will always remember with gratitude and a smile, my colleagues and others on the Department of Corrections staff whose friendship became so important. They helped keep up my morale in often difficult situations, as we all faced the same stressors. I also have never forgotten and remain grateful to some inmates--- the cadre members working in Seven Block who did all they could to provide me with their protection. And I give my belated thanks to one unknown inmate who probably saved me from serious harm as I worked in a subhall office.

In the present, I want to acknowledge that without Judy Krasnow's interest and encouragement, I might never have embarked on the project of sharing my prison experiences through the writing of this book. Thank you, Judy, for inspiring me, and for your wonderful friendship that began that day when I was taking your prison tour, and you discovered that I had begun work in an office in Seven Block some 38 years ago! I look forward to reading the book you are writing about the history of the Jackson prisons, and I hope your tours continue to entice the public to learn more about the subject.

For the hard part of putting the words I wrote into publishable form, I have depended on my good friend Nancy Pollok, who has been a part of my life since even before I dreamed of becoming a psychologist! She enjoys my mention of her in my Prologue as a "sometimes irritating young friend!" I couldn't have done it without you, Nanc!

I am very grateful to two other women who have also written of their years working for the Department of Corrections in Michigan. As I had hoped, about a year after I started work, more and more women were hired by the Department to fill various positions. However, both Tekla Miller, author of "The Warden Wore Pink," and Adria Libolt, who wrote "A Deputy Warden's Reflections on Prison Work," rose to positions of authority during the 1980's in what had been considered a male domain before the late 1970's. I left without having a chance to become acquainted with these two exceptional women. When I contacted them while completing this book, I was delighted to find that I could look to them for encouragement and guidance in completing my project. They also gave helpful suggestions during much-needed editing. I have come to truly value the friendship of these women who were pioneers in the field of corrections.

Last, but far from least, I thank my husband Bob Walsh for remaining supportive during this lengthy project. Together, we have helped each other clarify some of our thirty-five year old memories, for he is presently writing of his own experiences during his much longer time with Corrections as Administrator of Psychological Services. While my employment there ended with our marriage in 1978, his day to day sharing of events after that has helped keep my own recollections fresh. I consider our lasting relationship, that began in Seven Block so long ago, to be the best and most positive of the prison-related events that I have written about in my journal.

Prologue

I knew right away when I interviewed, that the job with the Department of Corrections was going to be a challenge, maybe even as great a challenge as raising four children had been! As I looked back, however, I was aware that during the years I'd treasured being a mom and a housewife, in a way I'd had a script to follow. I had been doing exactly what I'd learned was expected, which was all the things that a woman was supposed to do in those days. The job with the Department of Corrections (D.O.C.) was an unknown script for me, and actually, for any woman. As far as I knew, there were no role models for me to follow. I was middle-aged and newly a grandmother, and I'd just accepted a position to work inside the world's largest all-male, walled prison, as the first, and at this time, the only female psychologist! My office would be right in Seven Block, the location of the Reception and Guidance Center at the State Prison of Southern Michigan, where inmates entering the system go to be sorted out.

How had I come to do this, after having lived the accepted role of wife and mother for so many years? I believe there were three incidents that not only influenced me, but changed the course of my life. They all happened personally to me, but their timing coincided with current events that also inspired me, among them the civil rights and women's movements of the 1960's.

The first incident happened during a visit to my parents, when I accompanied my Mom to a meeting with a group of her friends. My sister, sixteen years younger than I and my only sibling, was attending college then, and Mom was expounding on all the good things she was accomplishing. One of the ladies apparently noticed that I was being left out of the conversation. She reached over, patted me on the arm and kindly said, "it's all right, my dear. Wouldn't you rather be the pretty one than the smart one anyway?" Her question, although perhaps insensitive, was a gift, for it started me thinking about who and what I was, and I found that I was not at all content with just being considered "the pretty one."

The second incident occurred during a casual conversation with a young friend who was attending college at the time, and whose rather radical ideas I found both intriguing and sometimes irritating! We had just left a choir rehearsal when she began questioning me about my beliefs. Her challenges to my responses finally led me to retort defensively, "Well, I'd rather believe it even if it isn't true." Later, I had time to think about what I had said, and its implications. Had I really meant that? Was I content with a hand-me-down belief system, or was I capable and knowledgeable enough to formulate for myself what I truly do believe?

The third important incident came about when I had descended into a depression. A friend kindly encouraged me to come with her to a weekend at a Methodist camp meeting, for she hoped it might help raise my spirits. I was not particularly interested in listening to the speakers who were scheduled, and the first one lived up to my expectations as a "Hell and brimstone" orator. At that point I was almost ready to leave and walk the many miles home, just to get out of that situation. But the last speaker, a black minister from Washington, D.C., had things to say that suddenly seemed so relevant to me that it was as though a miracle occurred that night! His words challenged me to change what needed changing, to take charge of my life, to develop fully and *use* the talents I had been given, and to do my best to be an influence for good--- I didn't sleep at all that night at the camp. At last I knew what I would do, the direction I wanted to take. I had decided that from now on, I would write my own script!

At breakfast the next morning I was able to get a seat beside the speaker, Dr. Ernest Smith. Suddenly I found myself quite tongue-tied and unable to formulate what I wanted to say! I was so nervous I even dropped my silverware on the floor. I'm sure it was obvious to him that his words had affected me deeply. He wisely suggested that it might be easier for me to share my thoughts by writing them down, and gave me his address. That was a wonderful insight, as I've always found I am more verbal when I express myself on paper. So I did write to him, and he replied, and this is how he became a long-distance mentor to me for a number of years. I will forever be grateful to him for his encouragement and his continuing challenges.

First, however, I knew it was up to me to face my immediate situation. Of course there was both consternation and opposition from my husband Maurice, when I announced my unprecedented plans to attend college. After all, we still had two children in high school. However, I was determined. Although it had been twenty years since I'd been in a classroom, I took a deep breath and tackled the college entrance tests, alongside the many young people just graduating from High School that year. I soon found myself enrolling in college as a freshman that fall, when my oldest son did also, at a different school. I had decided to become a psychologist (though the advisor said, "Don't you mean a social worker, my dear?") I was not to be deterred. For the next six years, I became immersed in the sheer joy of learning new things! I did well academically, too, and was proclaimed valedictorian of my class at Lansing Community College, thereby paving the way to full scholarships at Michigan State University and Central Michigan University for the remaining four years. I also managed to subdue my natural shyness, and began to make my voice heard in behalf of social causes and on issues I felt were important. I gained my master's degree in clinical psychology in 1973. Receiving that diploma ended one exciting and rewarding era in my life, one in which my script had included developing a new sense of independence and self-worth. However, I felt then that what I had accomplished was the attainment of an interim goal, and really was only preparation for what was ahead of me. I was right!

Although I had been flying high for six years, after school was over I was forced to face the fact that there was no great clamor for inexperienced psychologists to work in our immediate area. I enjoyed helping for a while in a Crisis Center not far from home, but it was only part-time employment, and when I was offered work with Social Services as a Research Analyst, I knew I had better accept. However, there I was in a cubicle working with numbers, not people. So all that year, I kept on applying for positions that were listed by the state, including one in the Department of Corrections (D.O.C.) that had to do with gathering data from various prisons. The D.O.C., however, informed me that I was not suitable for that work, as I would not be allowed to enter male prisons!

Then finally, there came notice of a job opening at the State Prison of Southern Michigan (SPSM) for a psychologist. I applied for it, and after an interview, was offered the position. With some trepidation, I accepted.

My two and a half years working there in Seven Block are what this book is about. Because I knew immediately that I was sure to have unusual experiences that I would never want to forget, I kept a journal of each day's events during my first six months in Seven Block. And after that, until I resigned from my position in 1978 following my marriage to a co-worker, Dr. Robert Walsh, I continued making brief notes that would remind me of events that happened, and the people involved, and my feelings and observations about them at the time.

I did return to a part-time position in the Psychological Services Unit for five and a half months in 1981, filling in for a therapist who was off on sick leave. However, the psychologists' offices had been moved out of Seven Block, and by then there were many women employed in the prison, in various positions. Fortunately for me, my employment in 1981 ended exactly one month before the devastating prison riot in May of that year!

Upon leaving in 1981, I stored away everything that had pertained to my work at "Jacktown," for I felt sure the gates had clanged shut behind me for the last time. I developed other interests, though I kept up on what was happening in the Psychological Services Unit through my husband, who continued as Administrator of Psychology at the prison until he retired after 25 years, in 1999.

Then just recently, we began hearing about tours of the Jackson prisons that included Seven Block! Now I had a chance to return once more. The day came when once again, I was actually standing and walking in Seven Block! The emotions I felt in that huge, five-tiered cell block were almost overwhelming. Perhaps it was from the realization that the bustling, noisy, odor-ridden, roach-infested Seven Block I remember no longer exists, that it is a part of history now. The structure is there, of course--- the building called the bubble, the bullpen, the ramp, and finally, the cellblock itself. But my mind began trying to reconstruct the scene as it had been, minus the current bright lights and color, but with the grimy darkness and the cacophony of sound and movement I had experienced each morning. Our offices have been converted back to cells on base and on the galleries. The concrete building that stood in the center of the block is gone. And gone too, are the people I knew then, the ones I cared about deeply, the ones I feared, the ones who helped me, the ones I tried to help--- It has been nearly thirty-five years! I found that my hands were shaking as I stood there.

I met Judy Gail Krasnow that day on the tour. It is she who developed and conducts the tours of the Jackson Prisons. Since we became acquainted, she has inspired me to recall how it was then, as the lone woman working in Seven Block. And she has encouraged me to share those memories not only with her, but also with all who are interested, through the writing of this book. She has become my good friend, and I am more than happy to share with her my memories about that time in Seven Block, all those many years ago.

I have been helped frequently, too, by my husband Bob, whose hiring by the D.O.C. predated mine by about nine months. My marriage to Bob coincided with the end of my career in corrections in 1978, but we still enjoy the reactions of new friends when we tell them that we first met in prison! I have turned to him many times during the writing of this book to confirm that incidents I am recalling actually happened as I remember them. He still encourages me to write, even though my household duties often fall to him when I just *have* to get something down or lose that thought!

This book is based primarily on my original six months of journal reports, followed by an expansion of the brief notes I made in the following two years. I've added a few words here and there to the daily journal entries, mostly to clarify prison nomenclature to the uninitiated, or to better describe the situation I had written about. I have not used the actual names of inmates, as I feel they have a right to some privacy, even at this late date. In most cases, I have also changed the names of prison staff and employees. Otherwise, this is a factual account of my time working in Seven Block and the State Prison of Southern Michigan.

WILLIAM G. MILLIKEN, GOVERNOR

CORRECTIONS
COMMISSION
Max Biber, Chairman
Duane L. Waters, M.D., Vice Chairman
Earnest C. Brooks
G. Robert Cotton, Ph.D.
Florence R. Crane

DEPARTMENT OF CORRECTIONS

PERRY JOHNSON, Director

State Prison of Southern Michigan
4000 Cooper Street
Jackson, Michigan 49201

September 10, 1975

Ms. Eugenia W. Becker

We are informed that you have successfully completed the qualifying examination and your name appears on the Civil Service Register awaiting an appointment to a position of ___PSYCHOLOGIST TRAINEE 08___

We have a vacancy in that class at this institution. If you are interested and wish to be considered for appointment, it will be necessary for you to appear for an interview.

Please report to the Personnel Office of the State Prison of Southern Michigan at Jackson, Michigan on WEDNESDAY, SEPTEMBER 17, 1975 at 12:30 P.M.

If for some reason you do not wish to be considered for appointment, please advise in writing. We will appreciate a prompt reply as there are others under consideration.

We are attaching an application which we ask that you complete and bring with you on the date of your interview.

Yours Very Truly,

Raymond H. Kraft
Personnel Officer

Figure 2 - Notification of a job – I must decide if I'm interested!

The Beginning

I guess the whole thing became real for me as I sat in the waiting room the day of the interview, anticipating that someone would soon acknowledge that I was alive and present. I'd checked in at the personnel office per instructions in the letter (the one I almost threw away without opening) and had been told to wait outside. So there I was, twenty minutes early, and feeling distinctly uncomfortable among the families waiting to see inmates. I couldn't shake the feeling that all those people were aware that I was "different," i.e., considering a job on the side of "law and order," while they were there to see brothers, sons, fathers, husbands, maybe lovers, who had transgressed society's rules to the extent that society felt better with them behind bars. And I was aware that right at that time, there was a color difference, too. I told myself that my awareness of this stemmed from guilt over having been born with the advantages of being white and middle class, rather than from any inherent racism in me. No, I certainly wasn't a racist! I had been appalled by the discrimination and racial hatred I saw when we lived in the south in the 50's, evidenced not just by the Klan, which was very active at the time, but even by our neighbors and friends there. It was this experience that had propelled me into activity when the fight for civil rights began in earnest. But I didn't know how to react to the small black boy lying on the seat next to me who kept kicking my purse (and narrowly missing my leg) or to the three young black men on the neighboring bench who seemed to be sizing me up. So I was relieved when a good-looking black man came out of the office and told me I hadn't been forgotten, but would be interviewed as soon as everyone came back from lunch. I returned to my wait, as the family of the small boy departed with him to regions as yet unknown to me. A shapely girl, with her blouse unbuttoned to the waist, sauntered along by the vending machines and again I felt "different," wearing a dress and jacket to achieve an altogether "sensible" appearance--- at least that was my impression of myself that day. I was even wearing the largely unused bifocals I hated so much!

Later

That was an interesting job interview. The first question shot at me by Dr. Houseworth was "Have you ever been raped?" With sheer will power, I refused to be rattled, and he seemed satisfied with my simple "No." The questioning went on from there about as I expected--- about my training, background, experience, knowledge of testing, and finally, my motivation (something of a stumper as I wasn't sure of that myself). There were four of us around a table: Dr. Houseworth, who, it seems, runs the psychological unit; the good looking man previously encountered was the Superintendent of the Reception Center; and Dr. Halstead, who apparently would be my immediate boss. I was somewhat surprised to see that Dr. Halstead has longish hair, a beard, and wears an earring. That didn't shock me, but it really didn't fit my concept of prison attire!

Anyway, I learned that if hired, I would be interviewing men who have just arrived to do their time in the system, and who need to be sorted out on a number of factors before being placed in one of Michigan's prisons. One of those factors is their psychological makeup--- there are quite a few very disturbed individuals who come through the system. I would also be conducting group therapy and probably evaluations for the parole board to peruse when making their decisions. When I considered all this, I thought, do I want this job?? Or even more to the point right now, will these three people decide that they want me? I really doubted that all this would come to be. As I look back at today's events, it all seems surreal. But I will wait and see---

Three weeks later!

Just when I had given up ever hearing whether I had survived the scrutiny of those three interviewers at the prison, I received a call from Dr. Houseworth, who proclaimed that I was the first choice of the committee. Would I start work in October? Truthfully, to say that I was the "first choice" would be a bit of a stretch, given that the amount of time that had elapsed gave them plenty of opportunity to be turned down by other candidates. But I ignored this and based my decision on just how willing I was to be (apparently) the first, and only female psychologist presently working behind the walls of Jackson Prison! I had much thinking to do prior to calling him back.

Decision time

Now that I've actually set foot in Seven Block, the location of the Reception Center inside Jackson Prison, I must make up my mind, and soon! It wasn't a long tour--- it really didn't have to be. Just standing there trying to take it all in was a unique experience. Seven Block is *huge!* The far end was almost invisible because of cigarette smoke as well as distance. As I looked up, I could see that it is many stories high, as well. The echoing noise from the inmates' constant talking, yells, and jeers made it hard to concentrate. Did I have an impulse to turn around and run? Yes--- but also, I was aware that I have been given the opportunity to enter a world that is foreign to most people. Knowing this does make it intriguing to contemplate working in such a setting. My husband says it has to be my decision. I am asking myself, do I have it in me to do this? When I applied last year for a job to do research for the Corrections Department, someone determined that I wasn't suitable to enter various prisons to collect information. I guess there is a part of me that says, "I'll show you!" And I feel sure, after having experienced a miserable year in a cubicle working on statistics for the Department of Social Services, that my training as a psychologist has to have equipped me to do something that is more meaningful! After all, isn't the desire to help others the reason I made the life-changing decision to start college after raising four children? (And I can always quit, right?)

Mid-October

I have decided to accept the position, and to keep a daily account of my activities while working at the prison. I am to start work next week. If all goes well, (meaning if I survive!) hopefully I will have a record of events set down on paper that someday will help me look back on an extraordinary time in my life.

Reception and

The beginning

Inside the Reception Services Unit where an average of 5000 new commitments and parole violators are received each year.

Used by courtesy of the Michigan Department of Corrections.

Guidance Center

The Reception and Guidance Center (R&GC) is the facility designated by the Michigan Corrections Commission to receive all male felons sentenced through the various judicial districts in the State of Michigan. It is physically part of the State Prison of Southern Michigan (S.P.S.M.), but is considered a separate facility dependent on the main institution only for auxiliary support. It is directed by a Superintendent who is responsible to one of Michigan's four Regional Directors. All felmale felons are received and processed in the new female institution at Ypsilanti, Michigan.

Like many other institutions, the Reception and Guidance Center has undergone a great deal of pressure with the increasing number of individuals sentenced. The number of men now received has nearly doubled since 1975. Under Michigan law, R&GC has no option but to receive all felons delivered by county sheriffs as long as the proper legal procedures have been followed. In addition to population pressures, the R&GC suffers limitations because it is a facility that was not designed initially as a reception center and is not ideally suited for clinical and diagnostic services. At the present time, the Department is planning to initiate a de-centralized reception service, with male felons above age 21 being received and classified at the present site at SPSM and all younger offenders being received at the planned Ionia Riverside Complex Reception Center. Persons sentenced in the upper peninsula may be received at the Marquette facility if placement there seems appropriate.

The Reception and Guidance Center is made up of two major subdivisions, the Reception Services Unit and the Psychological Services Unit. A third unit, the Psychiatric Services Unit is being shifted from R&GC administration to the Office of Health Care at the new Ionia psychiatric facility. The Reception and Guidance Center is responsible not only for receiving and processing individuals, but for coordinating their initial transfer within the Department. It is within the R&GC that each new felon is tested and evaluated and subsequently placed at an institution suited to his security and program needs.

RECEPTION SERVICES UNIT

The Administrator of the Reception Services Unit is accountable to the Superintendent of the Reception and Guidance Center. He is responsible for the lodging, housekeeping, and custody needs of the unit and supervises the identification and file preparation on all individuals sentenced to the Department.

Staff of the Reception Services Unit consists of custodial officers, reception and record office employees. Reception Service Unit employees are responsible for the physical processing of the inmate, the recording and/or initiating of information which is used in processing and programming, and for filing and reproducing information for Departmental use. The reception area starts the R&GC processing by receiving the incoming inmate and the forms and reports that have been generated up to the point of intake. Then the commitment process is started by logging the arrival of the inmate and by initiating the Basic Information Sheet which contains the time computation and other information necessary for processing. The Record Office receives the papers and forms for each inmate from the reception area. The paperwork is separated, sorted, and collected in preparation to go into the three folders which are initiated for the Central Office, Institution and Counselor. Subsequently, the Record Office will receive forms and papers for the folders, primarily from the Word Processing Center (WPC) and the processing from R&GC inside. The folders are forwarded appropriately as the processing is completed. The Record office is also responsible for developing

Figure 3 - Above and following 2 pages — Description and photo of Reception & Guidance Center from Department of Corrections' brochure.

other R&GC information such as the Daily Bulletin, a record of inmate reception and transfers.

The R&GC intake and administrative areas are critical in inmate processing because of the need for the generation of timely information produced for the permanent file which will be used throughout the corrections process. The receiving area is responsible for the initial physical processing and for initiating the commitment paperwork. The work done in this area must be done not only fast but accurately. Since processing at the Reception Center inside depends upon the paperwork being ready, the work being done by the Record Office and the Word Processing Center must be timely so that inmates can be processed through the Reception Center in less than thirty days. Please see Enclosure 2 for Reception Services Unit procedures.

PSYCHOLOGICAL SERVICES UNIT

The Psychological Services Unit is administered by an Administrator who, with the aid of a Chief Psychologist, supervises a staff of thirteen Psychologists and Social Workers, and two Testing staff. He is responsible for operational procedures within the unit, coordinates outpatient services conducted by unit clinicians, and supervises the testing, interviewing, and classification phases of the reception process. He is charged with the approval or disapproval of all institutional transfers and placement orders according to Departmental guidelines, serves as community and interdepartmental liaison, and performs as Acting Superintendent of the Reception and Guidance Center in the absence of the Superintendent.

The Testing staff within the Reception and Guidance Center is responsible for administering batteries of tests on men entering and exiting the system. Each man, after completing the initial resception process and being assigned housing within the Reception and Guidance Center, undergoes a battery of three groups of tests; psychological/emotional, educational, and vocational. These tests assist unit clinicians in selecting an appropriate rehabilitation plan as well as custody placement. Please see attached information concerning details of the testing procedure.

Following testing, the man is individually interviewed by a Psychologist or Social Worker who uses the clinical interview, test results, and all background information to prepare a transcase evaluation (see enclosure). The transcase is designed as a document that outlines the man's security as well as rehabilitative needs, and in a sense it is the "blueprint" for the man's complete rehabilitation program within the Department. The clinician has the responsibility of intertwining and combining all material to assist the Department in having a good understanding of each individual client and each individual client's needs. In addition, the R&GC clinician has the responsibility of offering parole contracts to those individuals who qualify. (See enclosures for information concerning parole contracts). After the transcase is completed, each inmate appears before the Classification Director and two Classification Committee members. It is this Committee's responsibility to select each man's proper level of security and to assign him to an institution as set forth by Department policy and Michigan law. The Committee reaches their decision by reviewing all records, the transcase, and also by interacting with the resident. Any deviation from the placement guidelines of the Bureau of Correctional Facilities is referred to the Deputy Director of the Department of Corrections for his review and approval.

Psychological Services Unit clinicians also provide psychotherapy at SPSM and other regional facilities based on the recommendations of staff clinicians as detailed in the transcase report. The psychotherapy groups are divided up into six broad categories which include groups for ambulatory schizophrenics, severe alcoholics, drug dependence, sexual offenders, individuals with impulse control problems and a general category of inadequate individuals. To assist in an equitible manner of placing individuals in therapy and to assist in keeping track of individuals as they move throughout the system, a centralized waiting list for psychotherapy has been established in the unit through the use of a computer. The demand for therapy has grown with the increased population with 241 individuals awaiting therapy in January, 1976, growing to a total of 1,101 as of April, 1977. The number of people in psychotherapy through the Reception and Guidance Center has grown from a total of 133 in January, 1976, to the present total of 479. The number of individuals in therapy at the present time is limited because of the shortage of clinical staff. In additin to preparing the transcases and doing psychotherapy, the unit clinicians are called upon to provide a range of services including crisis intervention, transfer evaluations, and psychological evaluations on request for the Parole Board. The number of the latter requests per month has gone from 138 in January, 1976, to its present level of over 272 per month in 1977.

The Reception and Guidance Center is also involved in a pilot program consisting of the assisgnment of individual clinicians to three of the largest cellblocks in the State Prison of Southern Michigan. The goal of this program is to assist the individual housing unit managers in dealf with the disturbed individuals within their cellblocks who are not ill enough to be transferred to the central mental health facility. This is an attempt to make available the expertise of trained mental health workers to assist both staff and residents.

In March, 1976, Exit Testing of the academic achievement of inmates immediately prior to their release to the community was initiated. The Testing Coordinator of the Psychological Services Unit was made responsible for coordinating the scheduling and administration of Exit Testing with the releasing institution treatment director and appropriate academic personnel.

JB/dmc

The Word Processing Center is responsible for typing administrative, operational, and personal paperwork for the Reception and Guidance Center. Emphasis is upon routine processing, generally consisting of clinician's clinical impressions and Classification reports. Other items, such as disciplinary hearings and personal correspondence are also part of the WPC workload.

First Day!

Monday, Oct. 20th 1975

I am up at six after a night of wakefulness. I was also fully awake at one and five-thirty. But it's hard to crawl out of bed. My breakfast consists of oatmeal and coffee (only a half cup--- would there be a ladies room in that all-male fortress?) I say goodbye to my husband, who's still in bed, at 6:50. Rain, dark, lots of traffic through Lansing--- not a fun drive. I arrive at the prison at 7:40 and, thankfully, have time to sit in my car for 10 minutes. A guard tells me to park in the visitors' lot today. It is just starting to get light as I go in to the personnel office in the main building. I ask for Dr. Houseworth, and am told to wait outside in the lobby. At 8:00, Dr. Halstead arrives and tells me Houseworth is at the dentist. He introduces me to Suzie, a friendly lady in personnel, who gives me forms that take me 1½ hours to fill out. The Superintendent arrives just as I'm finishing. He is very pleasant. Then there is another wait in the waiting room, so I cautiously venture into the visitor's john. It smells bad and there are no locks left on the stall doors.

Shortly, Dr. Halstead arrives and guides me to where I will be working. I have to leave my purse with a pleasant young lady in the "bubble," as the small building attached to the cell block is called. Then I go through several electronic gates and have my "mug shots" taken. Actually, it is a really good picture (I'm NOT wearing my bifocals). I can't tell the new employees from the new "residents" (which is what inmates are called, though I learn later that first time residents are called "fish"). They also make me a key for my office, and I am told to sit just past what they call "holding," which is where new resident arrivals await their sorting and processing through reception in the bubble. I sit in some man's chair, while my ID is being made. Then Dr. Halstead and I are buzzed through, and proceed down the tunnel, a lengthy ramp with an electronic gate at the bubble end, and a keyed lock at the cell block end. Both are locked and unlocked by guards peeping inside the ramp through small windows.

At last I am actually down in Seven Block. It's dark and murky and seems immense. There are hoots and whistles--- Dr. Halstead comfortingly tells me that they whistle at new residents, too. We proceed down the block for what only *seems* like a mile, past many cells and a small one-story building built right in the center of the block, containing offices of some kind. My office is right on "base" at the far end, and takes the space of two cells, I am told, the bars having been replaced by block walls, front and back. My new key opens the door. There's a small window with solid glass high in the door, and a hole with a ventilating fan in the back wall, which opens to the catwalk that runs between the cells and the outside wall of the cell block. The walls are painted blue, and for furniture, there is a desk and three wooden chairs. I'm told I have staff as neighbors in other converted cells nearby. And I'm warned to *always* keep my pass ID and keys with me. For my own safety, I am never to lock the door when I am inside.(?)

At this point, Dr. Halstead explains some of what is going on. As I knew, I will be interviewing inmates whose first stop in the system is here in quarantine, i.e., inmates while here to be screened cannot go elsewhere in the prison, and are restricted to this block. I will be doing psychological evaluations. I will also be responsible for recommending what type of programs a man would most benefit from, which prison in the system he should be sent to based on his history, and my prognosis of his future behavior, among other things. After I get used to doing up to eight interviews and dictating the eight evaluations each day, I will be expected to form and lead therapy groups *inside* the main part of the prison--- and oh yes, I will also be evaluating men who are coming up for parole. And there are other duties on Seven Block as well--- like assisting Mr. Ribby, whose job it is to classify men after they have been processed while in quarantine (which usually takes at least three weeks) and to tell them, one by one, where they will be serving the rest of their sentence.

Seeing that I am just a bit overwhelmed at this point, Dr. Halstead takes me next door and leaves me with Dr. Dubochek (later better identified as *Mr.* James Dubochek, or Jimmy) who kindly steers me around for most of the rest of the morning. I meet Dr. Hosner (I later learn he is *Mr.* Hosner, and I should call him "Lou,") and he is very friendly. He is an older man, while most of the others on the staff that I have met so far seem younger. I go up many flights of metal stairs on a tour of the block (it seems *very* high up there on fourth gallery!) Then we go back down to the little building, which is divided into three rooms, two used for psychological testing of the inmates, while the third is the office of the transportation officer, Mr. Earl Grier. Ah yes, the rest room. The door far across the cell block from my office says "Please knock," which is certainly a good idea, since I am the only woman working on Seven Block!

I am given tests to look over in my office, also other data and civil service papers, and information from personnel. After quite a while, I realize it must be noon, and I am hungry. I'm not sure just what I am supposed to do, but decide to be brave, so I go out of my office into the confusion and hubbub of the cell block. And yes, I do remember to take my pass and key, and I lock the door. But then I am unsure about where to go and start walking along the offices, when I bump into one of the other psychologists, who is walking the other way. He grins and says, "If you are going out to lunch, you are going the wrong way!" He guides me all along the block and through a door at the other end that leads into Six Block (the protection unit, he tells me.) We climb stairs and go through that block past cells on one of the upper galleries and then down again and out into a very large, busy, round area that my guide tells me is appropriately named the "Rotunda." Then I must get back outside the prison by myself, as he is headed elsewhere in this huge State Prison of Southern Michigan. I see the main electronic gate. I shakily show my pass as I go through and get no hassles from the officers there--- I guess I am clearly distinct from the inmates!

However, then I have to walk outside the building in the driveway to return to the bubble to get the lunch I had packed, and which I had to leave there with my purse this morning. I decide to eat in my car--- familiar territory! The egg salad sandwich tastes wonderful. After I relax a few minutes, I get out and there is Dr. Houseworth. He tells me to go back to my office by myself--- that I can go anywhere in the prison unescorted. (Do I really want to?? Several staff members told me I shouldn't!) I have discovered that there is a rest room in the civilian side of the bubble near the typing pool, and while there I meet Betty, a gal who seems very friendly. She tells me she wouldn't work inside, or even go *into* the cell block. This is *not* what I need to hear! I go past the typists, busy in a large room across from the Superintendent's office, and go outside again so I can go in by the same door to the bubble that new inmates enter. There I am allowed (buzzed) through several electronic gates. The photo man wants to know if I will

State Prison of Southern Michigan

When the State Prison of Southern Michigan (SPSM) was built in the 1930's the philosophy was to economically house as many prisoners as possible in one location. As a result, SPSM became the largest walled prison in the world, a distinction which still persists today. However, with the rise of modern-day philosophies, which call for treatment of offenders rather than soley imprisoning them, the size of the institution has become a detriment to corrections goals.

Two miles north of the City of Jackson, SPSM is divided into two large units, a maximum security facility and a trusty division. It is in these two units that nearly half of Michigan's 8000 to 9000 prisoners are housed. All are over the age of 23.

Attached to the maximum security facility, but not considered a part of it, is the Reception and Guidance Center. Dependent upon SPSM for some ancillary support, it is this unit where all new commitments are received for testing, evaluation and subsequently transferred to the institution best suited to their needs.

THE MAXIMUM SECURITY FACILITY

Inside 35-feet-high walls, the maximum security facility accommodates an average population of 2000 to 3000 residents in eight different, single-occupancy, cell-type housing units. Depending upon their needs, prisoners are daily involved in a variety of rehabilitation programs ranging from education and drug abuse treatment to religious activities and work programs.

Figure 4 - The prison is huge — I could have used a road map!

be there every day! I go toward the ramp alone and more raucous buzzers signal that I should be let through both locked ends.

Thankfully, once out of the ramp, Jimmy meets me in the block, and he invites me to spend the afternoon in his office. I am glad to do so, as he is very helpful. He has an evaluation scheduled and calls a man in from the benches that line the walls outside the psychologists' offices. During the interview, there is a "flap" over Jimmy's using the word "fuck"--- the inmate is very protective of me! He is twenty, which is just my youngest daughter's age. I begin to comprehend the amount of work I will be doing and feel tired already, and wonder if I'll hold up! I'm told I can't carry anything personal, even an aspirin, into the cell block, and I get the word about shakedowns and emergencies--- I leave a bit early, after chatting with Jimmy about my motivation, which is still a bit of a mystery to me, too. It is still a sunny day outside. I collect my purse and walk from the bubble hundreds of feet back to the main building, which houses the time clock on the "civilian" side of the main gate, and I am instructed on how to use it by putting a card in to be stamped with the time. I'm told I can check out at 4:25 each day, and I do so for the first time. But after driving the 44 miles home and arriving at 5:20, I am so very tired, and I see that my eyes look red. I tell myself, "One day at a time!"

Tuesday, Oct. 21st

I am getting the feeling that Dr. Houseworth is testing me--- he again insisted I walk among the inmates without escort. I ran into him this morning at the time clock, after a nice drive down 127. (I saw a fiery, red dawn.) Anyway, he left me to go through the bubble alone, but the guard there refused to let me go in unescorted. By then, Houseworth had caught up, and he walked down the ramp with me in silence. From Mr. Grier's office, I had to go it alone. Amid hoots, whistles and catcalls, I fumbled with the key to my office door, knowing that I often have trouble manipulating keys efficiently. My prayers are answered--- it opened on the first try!

Speaking of keys--- I admit that I really did panic for the first time, this morning. They had scheduled me to go outside of Seven Block, to the trailers in the prison yard that are being used temporarily as offices for other psychologists,

1 My office in Seven Block

2 The Bubble

3 Seven Block

4 Side entrance

5 Main entrance

6 Rotunda, Control Center

7 Five Block

8 Six Block

9 The Subhall

10 The therapy room (radio room)

11 Officer's Dining room (Rose Room)

12 Trusty Division

Figure 5 - Locations at the prison that I needed to know

and to watch the interviews conducted there with residents. I had no trouble leaving the block along with other staff, and the interviews were interesting. Then it was the time scheduled for me to meet with Bob Walsh, another psychologist, at his office next to mine in Seven Block, so I started back across the yard alone. Well, not alone, exactly, as there were quite a number of residents scattered about the area. I arrived at the cell block door just as the catcalls started--- and found the door was locked! Of *course* it was locked--- I should have known it would be! The fear I felt was really irrational, because I *knew* I had the key to that cell block door safely in my pocket. (A cool head is a necessity here!) Just then, Ethan Rycroft came along and helped me open it.

I ate lunch today in the lunchroom in the main part of the prison that has vending machines, and all the others eating there were men. Most of the seats were already full of hostile-appearing guards (officers), but I saw one black man alone at a table, and asked if I could sit there with him? He smiled and said "Of course!" and that was how I met Tyrone Marshall, who, I gather, has a position of some authority in Seven Block. He seems very nice.

However, while eating, we had to listen to one of the guards loudly complain that they never should have dismantled the "best" cell block, just because the do-gooders thought solitary confinement inhumane! I had heard about that block already. It was located out in the yard, and reportedly was infamous for the severity of the punishment which had been meted out there. However, I think his ranting today may have been for my benefit, as it's evident that many guards feel women have no place here. So far, I think I am as uneasy around the guards as I am with the residents, but I am hoping their apparent hostility will change after they get used to having a woman around.

Then I attended my first staff meeting, which was held in a room in the small building in the block. My, what a lot of dissension in the group! I was also shocked to learn of the staff's vulnerability to lawsuits. And I was doubly shocked to learn that inmate psychological services are almost non-existent at Ionia Max. Prison because of a lack of staff, with only one psychologist for thousands of inmates! So now I am wondering about SPSM. I suspect I will soon find out.

I also found myself feeling teary today, (I must toughen up!) while sitting in on Bob Walsh's interview of a young (18) inmate. He had a low IQ, and was scared half to death. According to his file and from what he told us, he had a bad time growing up, and I am wondering what kind of a system this is, that places a youngster like this in a place like the Jackson Prison Reception Center! I also sat in on a number of other cases. One man had formerly been convicted of homicide and was back again, one was in for rape, and so on. So far I haven't found it hard to relate to most, for on some level, as human beings, we share common experiences and emotions. It was more difficult with one latent psychotic, however, as his thinking process seemed different. Even he was interesting, as he had a low IQ and had to count on his fingers when asked how many brothers and sisters he had.

I like most of my fellow therapists so far. I sat and talked with Ethan for a while today before leaving. The bubble closes at shift change at 4:25 so you must get out, *and promptly*. It reminds me of Cinderella's midnight deadline! I *must* get a watch. I hear I'm to take a case Thursday by myself. And I observe Louis Hosner tomorrow. I wish I could look forward to each day, but so far there seem to be few rewards for doing this work. I'm having trouble sleeping--- I'm also trying to get in a car pool.

Wednesday, Oct. 22nd

I woke up very early again on my third day and started shaking. I felt even worse when I saw pea soup fog outside! I hurried to leave 15 minutes early because of it, and was upset with my husband for being so calm about it all. Actually, the fog was gone by the time I got to U.S. 127, so I was plenty early. The sky was streaked with red and the trees stood out, silhouetted against it among ghostly patches of fog. I had to go into the block and all the way to my office alone this morning, so I moved fast, as there are always many inmates milling about in the cell block. I spent a few minutes sitting in my office to calm down before venturing out to find Hosner's office. I went up the stairs to the second level (which is "first gallery") without locating it, and returned to Mr. Grier's office to ask our clerk, Mark, where to go, and he escorted me back up to second gallery.

I've heard plenty of pros *and* cons about Hosner already, but I will say, he truly is unique! It was interesting to see how he handles the residents--- trying to do a bit of "therapy" with each, apparently. He uses a whole bag of tricks, from name-calling to sermons to puzzles and teaching, within minutes! I saw my first lifer today. Actually, he had two life sentences. He had robbed and then butchered an old couple who were friends of his family! There were also some sad cases--- young kids who never dreamed of such big trouble. Hosner works fast, so there was time before lunch for me to go back to my office.

I still don't have a watch, and soon began calling the psychs in other offices, but no one answered. So I started out on my own, and this time I was glad to run into Don Houseworth by Grier' office. He said he'd take me up to lunch in the Officer's Dining Room (OD), which we reached by going through 6 block and then all the way down the long subhall swarming with inmates, and finally, after a guard's hostile scrutiny of my pass, up a small stairway at the end of the subhall to the OD. The trip there feels like--- and is--- a journey into the depths of the prison. The food was pretty awful, but it's nice to relax with other staff and even be served ice cream for dessert--- all free! I had time for a more friendly conversation with Houseworth (he's the boss, but everyone calls him "Don"), and found myself telling him about not being able to sleep, and so on, and ended up asking him why he had hired me? He gave me some good answers, about how men shouldn't be segregated from all contact with women, I had good credentials, and they also wanted a mature person---

Then I sat in with Paul Wittenberg in the afternoon. He's not dramatic, but is a nice young man, and he taught me a lot of basics. He fixes the only good cup of coffee, too, with an immersion heater. He invited me to join their car pool from Lansing, and so I will, tomorrow. I get my first case tomorrow, too!

Mark made me a sign for my door today: "Mrs. Becker, Psychologist." Now I've arrived!

I had a struggle trying to get a dictaphone tape onto the machine this morning, and finally discovered one was already on! I've never had to use a dictaphone before and will admit it intimidates me.

I was nearly too late to get out via the bubble tonight! I guess I must look tired late in the P.M. Paul Wittenberg thought I was crying!

Thursday, Oct. 23rd

I slept better last night, so the morning didn't appear quite so bleak at first. I drove the ten miles in to Frandor shopping center in Lansing to meet Ronald Halstead and Paul by 7:05. I sat in the back seat and not a word was spoken until we arrived at the prison. Silence seems to be the unwritten rule. I didn't mind, and rested, at least. Then I went to the records office next to the

Superintendent's office and across from the typists in the bubble, to pick up the folders on my first case, as instructed. I couldn't find mine at first, but when I did, I felt like an old pro! I walked in through the ramp with a group, and was greeted in the block with catcalls and obscene comments that seemed worse than usual. I was allowed to carry in a cup, my alarm clock, a poster and various folders, and also a picture of Chris, my little grandson. I borrowed scotch tape from Bob Walsh to hang my poster, which is an undersea scene, which is what it feels like in my office with no real windows, far down on base in the block.

Then I joined Bob in his office for a morning of interviews. One was a thoroughly unlikeable "Joe Cool"--- most have been either pathetic or superficially likeable--- but not this one! I also talked some with Bob, who told me about the rampant drug and alcohol use (the booze is made from potato peel and rubbing alcohol) in the prison. Also, he said that homemade knives abound. Thanks, Bob! We ate lunch together, but I already had a super headache, and of course, no aspirin! We parted after eating, so I could go to the "ladies" in the bubble, as I refuse, thus far, to knock on the men's room door on base in Seven Block, in view of 500 inmates! So once again, I had to walk back in and down the ramp alone.

I skimmed the files for a while, then opened my door and called my first case to come in. Luckily, he was a very likeable guy, but as I hear is often the case, he swears he was framed. He was also very talkative. After he left, my head was still splitting, and since Bob had said Hosner had an aspirin supply, I called him and he said come on up. Well, I hate those stairs at the far end of base out of sight of the guards, but I went up, and he gave me three aspirin from his stash. He also gave the resident who was with him some! I went back down (amid comments from inmates that are not repeatable) only to find that my key wouldn't open my office door this time, and worse, wouldn't come out of the lock! Finally a young resident offered to help, but couldn't get it out either. So without thinking, I asked him to watch the key while I went to get Earl Grier to open the door. *He* had no trouble---how embarrassing! I now realize that it was a serious error to leave the key with the inmate, but no one chastised me for it--- yet. Then I realized I had no water to get the aspirin down. I finally felt so bad I gagged it down, as I certainly didn't want to lock that door again right away! But I still felt awful - just couldn't get it together. Lou came down to see how I was, and while he was there, Don Houseworth stopped in--- told me I was "anxious"--- ha! What a help that was! By then I was not only "anxious" but also panicky, because it was late, and my report wasn't dictated yet. And then I couldn't get the ****** dictaphone to work! I called Bob for help, but he was terribly busy. I actually called him twice--- and he finally did come over and helped me get it started. By then, it was 3:00, and we must be out by 4:15 of course, or get locked in. I barely made it today, and hardly remember what I said in the report. I may do it over again tomorrow. I still felt awful on the way home, but luckily, Ronald was driving. The air in the office probably didn't help my head. It really is terribly stuffy in that small, enclosed space.

We got to Frandor before I realized I'd left our alarm clock in my office, and that my daughter had borrowed my credit card and the gas gauge in my car read "empty!" An appropriate end of a perfect (perfectly awful) day!

Friday, Oct. 24th

I had used a small alarm clock last night because I left mine in my office at the prison yesterday. (I *must* take time to shop for a watch that works, *soon!*) So when I woke up feeling as though it was morning, I glanced at the clock and thought it said twenty of *seven!* Panic, as I have to meet Ronald and Paul at 7:05 at Frandor and this was *my* first day to drive! I dashed around like crazy, grabbing clothes, etc.—and when I finally went back to look at the clock again, it said twenty of *six!* Oh well. I got to Frandor early and got us to work on time.

I picked up files in the records office, said "Hi" to the typists, then went back outside as usual and into the other part of the Bubble where the "cage" is located. The cage, or bullpen, is a large, cell-like area where men newly arrived from around the state are placed prior to being processed (showered, deloused, photographed, given prison blue uniforms and their records checked for various problems) and which we go past in order to reach the ramp to enter the block. When I got to that area today, I found it was "shakedown" day. There were two troopers standing there! And this would have to be the day I tried to sneak a piece of candy into the block, in my pocket. However, the troopers told me I could go on in--- I guess I don't look dangerous.

Figure 6 - I passed by the "cage" or "bullpen" each day when going through the Bubble, before being buzzed to enter the ramp leading to Seven Block

I interviewed two men today, one in the morning and one after lunch. You have to know which man you are to see when, as the officers unlock the men when they are scheduled to be on call. The morning man really tried to con me. His record was monstrous, with many assaultive crimes, and all his psych tests looked faked. And he lied about everything! I didn't antagonize him, but did put him down as a poor security risk. My dictaphone is *not* working right, for I get echoes. Don stopped in to see how I am doing. Nice of him, but I must remember he is boss of all of us psychs, and I surely didn't act very professionally yesterday.

Dr. Chakraborty, an Indian gentleman and fellow psychologist, also stopped in briefly. I was busy going through files, so I called him back later. He had arranged with Paul to go out to a restaurant for lunch. Of course, he had to ask me along, and I accepted. (But I had to borrow some money to pay for the meal.) I drove, with Paul directing me, and we ate at a lovely place. But it took ages and I was on edge, as all three of us were gone 1½ hours! I felt like a truant, going back inside late!

45

I saw one young fellow this afternoon. Nothing spectacular, so I actually had time to read Don's book of policy. I kept my door open today occasionally, to keep the air moving. That felt better, but I was still too warm. On the way home, the fellows directed me a different way, and I made a bit of a mess of the driving. I also found out that Paul can't get three of us in his Corvette. So he may drive my Dodge Demon on his days, and pay me for the gasoline.

The typists are very nice, and often speak to me specially, as I go by to the records office. I think everyone believes something terrible is going to happen to me. I guess I do too, underneath. But I hold my head up high and walk normally. If a resident in the block says "Good morning," I reply, but not if they say, "How are YOU, baby?!"

Monday, Oct. 27th

Another week has begun. It's lighter in the morning now because of the end of Daylight Savings Time. But now it's nearly dark before I get home. Paul drove my car today and it's good to relax and leave it to him. I'm to figure out charges--- gasoline and oil, etc. The guard wasn't going to let me into the bubble this morning, and growled, "Where are *you* going, Maaamm?" so I flashed my ID (now worn on a leather strap on my wrist with my keys). Paul keeps telling me I should never go in alone--- but it's hard to do anything else, when no one on the staff is around.

I had two cases today, and managed with time to spare and then some. Both were interesting and both were schizophrenic to one degree or another. However, often the tests look much worse than the individual does as he presents himself in the interview. The one this afternoon--- well, I looked at the tests and read the record in the file, and decided to get on with the interview immediately, before I had time to get scared! The guy had hitched a ride, forced his benefactor into the trunk after robbing him, and later attacked him with a knife--- nice guy! At any rate, he wasn't that bad to interview.

This noon Paul walked me out and up to the Rose Room (OD) for dinner. It's called the Rose Room because of a lovely mural on the wall that was painted by inmates. Paul has been really nice about showing me the ropes. But we discussed my having to depend on everyone to walk with me wherever I go, and though he insists it's necessary, he doesn't really "not mind," I'm sure, and I can't blame him. The food was bad, as usual. I choked on the dry cake, and Paul advised putting milk on it. The resident who serves us on the line seems to enjoy giving me *big* portions, which I usually get only halfway through!

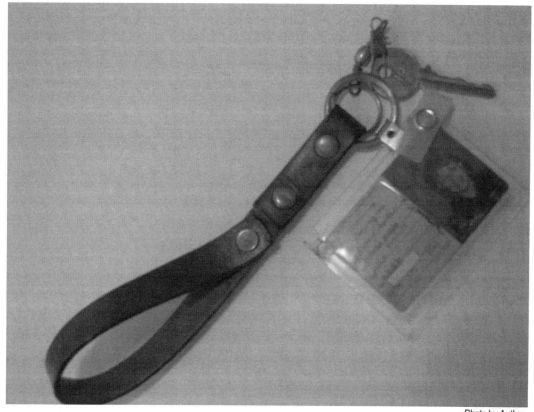

Figure 7 - I wore this leather wrist strap with ID pass and key attached for 2 1/2 years while working in Jackson Prison.

Ronald and Houseworth both mentioned that my first report wasn't bad. I went back over it and began to think so too! I also felt good about the reports I did today. The dictaphone quit talking back to me *at all* (!) so I did the afternoon report in writing. Then I had to make a trip up to the bubble with the dictaphone. Going through the block didn't seem too bad today. Maybe the men are getting used to seeing me. Anyway, there are a lot less of the gross noises now.

Paul tells me the guards never greet him "good morning" the way they do me! They are so concerned about me falling on the slippery floors. The mops are always busy at 8:00 and it's like walking on grease. *Some*day I'll probably be in a hurry, forget, and land on my fanny! The noise was deafening in the block after I arrived in my office, and Bob stopped over to explain that the banging was the authorities "testing the bars." BANG BANG BANG! Since I have been told that the cell locking mechanisms are so old they can easily be popped open, I wonder why the fuss about the strength of the bars!

I still only have two cases, but it's a good thing, as I just got my dictaphone back this afternoon. I'm beginning to feel quite the professional! I like to ask advice sometimes, though, and I dropped into Bob's office next door late this morning. That's when I found out there was a staff meeting this noon, so I went to lunch early, with Bob, at 11:00. Houseworth and Todd Miller (who is the testing director) were there in the OD also. Houseworth seems very reserved and lonely. It was bad food again, of course. The guards didn't question me today, in fact, the one who stopped me on the way in yesterday, apologized for it today.

Whenever I go through the upper gallery in Six Block on the way to the OD to lunch, I've noticed a small, older resident, who seems traumatized by my presence. He flattened himself against the wall in his cell and appeared frightened, the first time I walked through. I know Six Block is a protection unit and that there are homosexuals housed there also. Today he murmured "Hi" as I passed, and I answered and smiled. What does it mean to him, I wonder?

The staff meeting was a mess, with everyone disagreeing with everyone else! It really is too bad. I guess it's because there are a mix of so many different personalities. Ronald is friendly, a bit far out (with the one earring), and seems a little hard to get to know. But then, he's the boss, though he answers to Houseworth. Then there is Bob, who is always helpful. He has an infectious grin, but seems a bit self-conscious about his turned-out eye. Jimmy is very verbal, seems sure of himself, and is fun to be with. He appears to relate well with street people. Frank seems businesslike and efficient. Ethan comes across as sensitive, someone you can be yourself with. Dr. Chakraborty is middle-aged and has a thick accent (Indian) and is a gentleman who tries to make you feel at ease. Lou Hosner is certainly egocentric, and has a dry humor. He also has a bad temper, and it's hard to know how to take him. I gather that he has been working here for a *very* long time! Paul is a conservative southerner, though without visible prejudice. He works hard and is not aggressive. Dr. Houseworth is a small-statured man who seems reserved and authoritative, and probably is very "brainy." All of my descriptions may change, of course, as I get to know the other PSU staff better. The talk at the meeting was about all the new duties soon to befall us. Most of the psychs are upset about more work and think our talents could be put to better use. I am too new to have much of an opinion yet.

I am taking my notes home to destroy, as I don't trust the resident who empties my wastebasket (a cardboard box). I worry about leaving anything in my office, too, since the lights are left on at night to discourage residents from having sex in the offices! I also feel uneasy dictating reports when I know I can be overheard through the ventilating fan. Paranoid? Who, me?? I just discovered today that our helpful clerks who give the psychological tests to the inmates, are inmates themselves! They wear street clothes, not "blues" so I had no way of knowing.

Oh, a group of residents came to my door today. They had been told by someone that they were to see the psychologist, but I found that no one had them assigned. Maybe it was real and maybe not--- at least I tried to straighten it out. More and more residents speak politely now. There was a letter in the Spectator (inmate newspaper) today appreciating the fact that women are now working inside. I never have seen any, though I hear there are some nurses working in the infirmary.

I arrived at the time clock early tonight, as usual. But so did almost everyone else on the staff! So we stood around in a group, laughing about how the clock stands still when you watch it!

I'll bet I get more cases tomorrow.

I'm only assigned two cases again, which is really nice, because I have time for the many other things I need to do and learn. But I know it won't last.

This was my day to drive. Horrors! Only three trips on a tank of gas! Paul showed us a jack-o-lantern he had carved. He said it reminded him of home.

Today Bob showed me how to get to the OD for lunch by going through the yard. I don't think I want to try it by myself, though! We ate with Jimmy and several others.

I had an interesting case this afternoon, a typical sociopathic personality disorder, full of smooth talk, charm, flattery, and pseudo-insight--- It was hard not to fall for it, at first, but I had seen plenty in his file about his connections with organized crime. And then he began spelling out his immediate expectations of unrestricted telephone privileges, consults with his lawyers, and so on. I broke it to him that it just is *not* going to happen, while he is in quarantine!

I finished up early, and decided it might be a good time to call Ethan to see if I could tour "Top Six," the psychiatric clinic, known as the Clinical Services Unit, or CSU. He didn't answer the telephone, but before long, he popped in and said Bob told him I'd been trying to get hold of him. So he escorted me up to Top Six. The only way to get there is by one elevator in the main part of SPSM. Once up there, I talked with Mr. Monroe, who had George Bowman, an MA psychologist who works up there, show me around. All the patients locking there are psychotics, and there are hundreds. I wasn't allowed to see one section, because the men were taking showers (there was much joking about that!) But I saw the "solitary" cells with just mattresses, and a hole for a john--- and one with not even that. I was told to stay on the opposite side of the hallway from the cell doors, even though only a small area of each door is open (with bars.) Apparently you never know--- and further down, the doors were all sealed. Prisoners might throw things--- like feces. I also saw a crafts class doing ceramics, and the day room with a TV. I was shown a cell where an inmate just about burned himself up when he set fire to his mattress. It is really a terrifying place. I had to have someone walk both ahead of me and behind me. I was told that I will be able to see the rest tomorrow.

There are cockroaches and mosquitoes all over my office! And hundreds of pigeons outside, and sometimes inside, too! I'm told that inmates break the glass in the windows beside the catwalk.

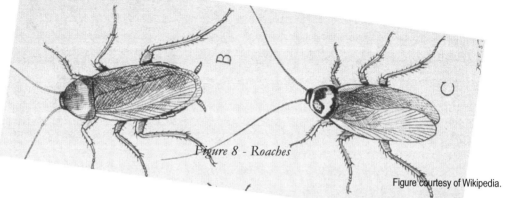

Figure 8 - Roaches

Figure courtesy of Wikipedia.

There was much more noise as I walked on base today--- a bit more frightening. I tried to go back out to the bubble by myself once, today, but no guard was there to open the ramp, so I had to walk all the way back to the clerks' office, and Dan (one of our clerks) phoned Control to let them know I was coming to be let out of the block.

Ronald complimented me on the one report he'd had time to read so far, said it was "A-OK." Tomorrow I'm to go to Trusty Division with Paul.

Bob says there's considerable feuding among staff members. It certainly shows in staff meetings. I haven't figured it all out yet, but there seems to be much resentment of Don Houseworth, as well as childish in-fighting involving several of the others.

Thursday, Oct. 30th

Well, today was not overtaxing. I was scheduled to spend the morning at Trusty with Paul, so we drove right over after arriving. The facilities there are nice and new and modern--- what a contrast! We interviewed three residents while there, mostly parole problems. One man was in for incest with a stepdaughter in her early teens (with his wife's permission!) He was furious with Paul for denying his parole. Actually, Paul had recommended therapy, which would flop his parole for now. The man threatened to sue Paul. Interesting. We also saw a young rapist. After all that, we ate lunch in the dining room over there. We were served at the table, and the food was *good!* It was a pleasant meal for a change. I left

Paul there and drove back to Seven Block after lunch was over, and distributed my reports. Then I went back to my office to wait for Mr. Monroe—who never showed up. Ethan did call me to tell me Monroe had another meeting. So I got on with my one case. After dictating, I had extra time so I wrote some letters.

I shut my finger in the car door on the way home tonight. Am I getting masochistic or what?

Friday, Oct. 31st

Today was still one and one cases and was relatively uneventful except for noon. I really hate to keep asking someone to escort me to lunch, and decided to try going on my own. I wasn't very hungry, so went up the ramp, through the bubble, and to the main waiting room in the prison. There I consumed a candy bar and a banana I had brought with me. I ate them in the ladies room. But I knew that really wasn't enough food--- and all I had with me were pennies (no paycheck yet!) So, I headed for the OD, alone!! I got through the main gates, past the rotunda, past the guard at the crosswalk, and all the way down the subhall to the stairs, before a guard stopped me, and did he ever give me a dressing down for being alone! I finally did get to go up the stairs, and ate at a table alone. I had a pork patty in front of me that was half raw, so I didn't eat it, but I did get a piece of pumpkin pie down. I was finishing a cup of coffee (part chicory, they tell me) when Don came along. And *he* told me I shouldn't come alone to eat!! (And who was it who told me on my first day that I could go anywhere in the prison unescorted??) He suggested I call *him* from now on. We did visit awhile before heading back, but I felt well chastised by then, for my daring.

It's Friday of week two! I heard Frank complaining on the way out that the trouble with Friday is that you have all weekend to dread Monday!

Monday, Nov. 3rd

Today I had 2 and 2 cases assigned, but it turned out to be 1 and 3, because some tests for one man hadn't come back yet in the morning. At least it was interesting today. I was busy every minute! One young man had a low IQ, was a neglected child, and is a still-unloved eighteen-year old. I could cry--- but know better! One man was manic (I labeled him cyclothymic) and the other man was a forty-one year old college graduate who was earning over $50,000 a year before he lost it all and began forging checks. He declared he had worked for President Nixon and got caught up in the Watergate mentality! Fascinating guy--- good looking, too--- but how much can you believe?

This noon I called poor Paul again (sigh), and we went to the OD and ate so-called spaghetti together. The best part about eating there is the obvious pleasure it gives the three regulars who serve me! I'm feeling a bit more at ease on the cell block now. More men speak to me, too.

I read the files, completed the interview and dictated the tape, all in one hour today. So Ronald says Wednesday I'll get three and three--- ouch! He said not to feel bad, I won't get that every day. No, the other days it will be four and four! I hope they are mostly first-timers (an A prefix on their files)! Repeaters with B, C, and D prefixes sometimes have files that are several inches thick, and I must be familiar with what is in them as well as in the current reports and test results, before doing the interview. It can mean a *lot* of reading! I can speed read, but just might miss something important if I do.

Tuesday, Nov. 4th

Today was a dilly! I had stomach cramps so hadn't slept well, and was glad Paul was driving. It was rainy and dismal, too. I was given two cases this morning. The first one went smoothly. But the second man was psychotic and talked of hearing voices telling him they are going to kill him. He stared at me constantly with expressionless brown eyes. Unnerving. While I was deliberating what to do, Ethan dropped by to see if I wanted to go to lunch. So he helped me with forms for getting the man sent to Top Six, and later I had to go to Control on first gallery to see about it. In the meantime, I went to lunch with Ethan, and then to staff meeting. It was the same old routine. No one will work with anyone on anything. And there was no end of bickering. I finally walked out! It all revolved around getting a better system of report distribution--- which we badly need.

This afternoon was training for new people. A new man was there too--- and seldom said a word. He doesn't even smile! We learned about all the other institutions in the system first, and later Steve Ribby told us about court sessions held in Seven Block. It seems we are called on to serve as advocates to represent residents who have committed rule infractions in Seven Block, when their cases are heard before a three-man custody panel in the classification office. I certainly dread that duty. We were also warned about not losing our keys. I am to keep them on me always (they are a bother, on that thick leather strap on my wrist with my ID).

Some of the things said in staff meetings make it apparent that there is a great deal of deep-seated hostility among several individuals on the staff, and often it quickly degrades from work-related discussion to personal attacks that are unprofessional and immature. I try to stay out of it as much as possible. This is a crazy place to work, indeed!

On the way out tonight the Superintendent stopped me and several others on the staff to meet the new candidate for a psychologist position. I tried to be friendly, but she ignored me completely. Needless to say, I'd rather she wasn't the one to get the job--- but she probably will.

On the other hand, it really *would* be nice to have another woman working nearby on the block! Would they get us a ladies room then, I wonder?

Wednesday, Nov. 5th

Today was really something else (have I said that before?) I had *six* cases, and I actually finished on time. Plus, I had the new man (also named James, so I will refer to James Dubochek as Jimmy) observing me in the afternoon. (I wonder if the woman I met turned down the job?) Actually, James was a help--- he's very good with the inmates. He got one man (a real con) to open up, and his was quite a story. I couldn't have done the interview as well as James did. My first case this morning was a young man who'd committed a brutal rape. I had a few qualms, but waded in and the interview went OK.

Dr. C. (everyone calls Dr. Chakraborty "Dr. C.") dropped in at noon and asked me to go out to lunch with him. I'm becoming impressed with him--- his knowledge, his kindness--- He gave me a copy of a book of poems he wrote. Apparently he's published many books. We had a very nice talk. He feels as I do about departmental friction. And he also had doubts about the gal we met yesterday who was in line for a job in the Reception and Guidance Center (R&GC).

Ronald told me tonight that Houseworth asked him how the new people were doing, and that he told him my work was excellent--- and that Houseworth replied that he'd read my reports and found them very good! I felt great--- but know I'll be making many mistakes along the way.

Thursday, Nov. 6Th

Every day is different. This morning I was assigned to outpatient services, which I had no idea how to handle. This unit needs better training for new people! One of the residents I had to see was the guy I sent up to Top Six before, and George Bowman had sent back promptly, without any treatment. So I sent him up again. Probably I will make enemies. But it's my professional judgment versus theirs. I also saw the man (the real con with mob ties) again, and got a different impression this time that made me uneasy. I also disagreed with Lou about one of his men. Well, I'm here to do a good job, not to be a yes-man (woman)!

Ronald tells me I'm the only therapist James (the new man) will open up with. James volunteered to walk me up to lunch today, and we stopped for a moment to visit with his sister Sara on the way. She is now in an office near the rotunda. Apparently she was in Seven Block briefly before I came on board. She says she has the same escort problems I do.

This afternoon I saw three men, and two were murderers. One, age 35, had gone berserk and on a shooting spree--- killed a dog, shot up a house, shot a man in the leg, and later shot him at close range with a shotgun. And yet I really felt I developed some rapport with the guy. Then next was a black 20 year old, who had shot his father. He came in singing! I think he is scared under it all. He has a life sentence.

I drove today, and always am more tired on my driving days. So far I've never had to put any of my cases on recall, but I do feel I'm too rushed to do some men justice, too. It's a dilemma. At times on the drive home I'll get sudden brainstorms as to what makes a man I've seen "tick."

Friday, Nov. 7th

Is it Friday again so soon? And yet I felt awfully apprehensive about today, and mentioned it in the car to Ronald. He helped me sort out my feelings, and what caused them: First, the increasing familiarity of many of the men I see, such as their asking about me, my family, and my being there at the prison. One guy yesterday showed me his tattoos (minus shirt), one mentioned he hadn't been alone in a room with a woman for a year, and asked if I was married--- Second, the whistling has increased when I am out of my office. These things aren't necessarily bad, I guess. Ronald says probably some of it's because I feel more at ease. (?)

Well, I did a parole evaluation at Trusty today. I *hate* it! They couldn't find an empty office for me over there, so finally they put me and the man I interviewed in a small room used as a cleaning closet!! It's obvious how much value is placed on psychologists over there! However, I managed to do the interview and then headed back to Seven Block to dictate the report. Bob had helped me a bit, earlier, by telling me what I should look for. The whole process took a lot of time. I hope I did OK. I granted the man an out, conditionally. It's a big responsibility, though of course the parole board has the final say, after they read my report.

After that, my first case was a kid I can't forget. He was 19 and so scared. He's always been told he is retarded, and has withdrawn from hurts to the point where I saw him as latent schizophrenic. And now he's being terribly sex pressured on the upper galleries. I spent a lot of time talking with him and then talking with colleagues about him. So finally I went to the Control desk and asked that he be taken off fourth gallery and locked near the desk on base, for protection.

I bumped into Frank outside my office, and he gave me the news then that an emergency alert was on because of trouble elsewhere. Thank goodness it is elsewhere! But that means we are restricted to the block until it is over. It's a good thing I came back from Trusty when I did, as the gates are locked, with no one let in or out, during an emergency. So four of us gathered in my office and we discussed my last case, which was helpful. After a while, Dr. C. and I decided to eat lunch right there on the tables where the men (who were in lockdown) in Seven Block eat, since we were hungry and couldn't leave. The food someone brought us wasn't bad! After we finished eating, I went to the desk and asked to see my last case again. When he arrived, I told him I was recommending that he be placed in Six Block for protection, when he is classified, and his face shone, he was so relieved. Now I just hope that that, or something similar, comes to be, and that classification agrees with me.

I also ran into the schizophrenic I sent up to Top Six for the second time yesterday, and he stopped me with a smile on his face (the first I'd seen from him!) He wanted me to know he finally got his medication and wanted to thank me for it.

Then I received a note (called a "kite") in my box in Grier's office from my check-forging friend the other day, expressing thanks for my dedication. Very nice of him, I think. Also manipulative, probably! But it made me feel good.

Then I saw two more cases. One was a depressed black kid who related to me like I was his mother. I spent extra time with him. And then, just before four o'clock, the desk called me to take care of an emergency. This was another referral to Top Six. So at the end of the day, I was so rushed, I thought I'd be locked in, for sure!

I talked with the guys a lot on the ride home, trying to come back down.

Monday, Nov. 10th

I began to think, this morning, that I was being tested to see if I could take it! The first man I was scheduled to see was in Top Six. So I called Ronald to see what he wanted me to do (hoping he'd say "forget it") but he told me to call and talk with the man's therapist, up there, to see if the man could be seen, and then to get back with him. So I did, and yes, I could, so Ronald and Paul stopped for me on their way to group. They *were* going to leave me at the SPSM elevator, but then Ronald relented and escorted me on up to the desk at Top Six. Then I had to wait to see the therapist, and in the meantime, was given a *real* cup of coffee, made from bottled water, not from the awful tap water like in R&GC. Finally, the therapist arrived with my case, a very subdued man of 30. We were escorted to eight different rooms, before one was found that was OK--- one was too cold, one was being used, etc. Then came the interview. I had ascertained by then from the files that he was a genuine split personality--- one a good father, but also one who rapes his daughter, beats his wife, and so on. Fortunately, I was interviewing the good guy, and the other didn't appear.

Then I went back down the elevator and traipsed outside all the way to the bubble and Seven Block. My next case there was a 17 year old who had received a 20-40 sentence for a kidnapping and rape which was very brutal. As far as I could see, the kid had no redeeming features, though he tried to "act good" while denying his guilt. He had only contempt for the girl who was the victim.

I had two lunch escorts today--- Don and Paul, and we sat at a table together. It was very nice, though I would have preferred to talk with each individually. The food was better than usual--- I didn't even find any ashes from the server's cigarette!

It was a more routine afternoon, except that I spent about half an hour talking with the gal who is the prospective staff member. I gave it to her straight about the conditions here. She's really undecided. Later, both Ronald and Don asked my opinion of her. She has more depth than I thought at our first meeting, but to me, doesn't seem right, somehow, for the job. Time will tell, if she takes it. Dan, one of our nice young clerks (they are called "cadre") called also, about getting the psych files in on time at noon. He apologized for bugging me! Jimmy dashed in for a brief chat, too. He agrees about the childishness of our staff meetings. Dr. C. stopped to escort me out tonight.

Wednesday, Nov. 12th

Today was not memorable except that I felt quite inadequate. I did six evaluations, and all seemed to be young black men age 21, and high on the Pd scale (psychopathy.) Thus, they began to blur together, and I hate to have that happen, as it's not fair to them. I also got back some of my reports that were not good at all. Oh, I did see one white man, and he refused any help. "No" to groups, high school classes, and so on. He was depressed, and stopped in later to

A kite I received.

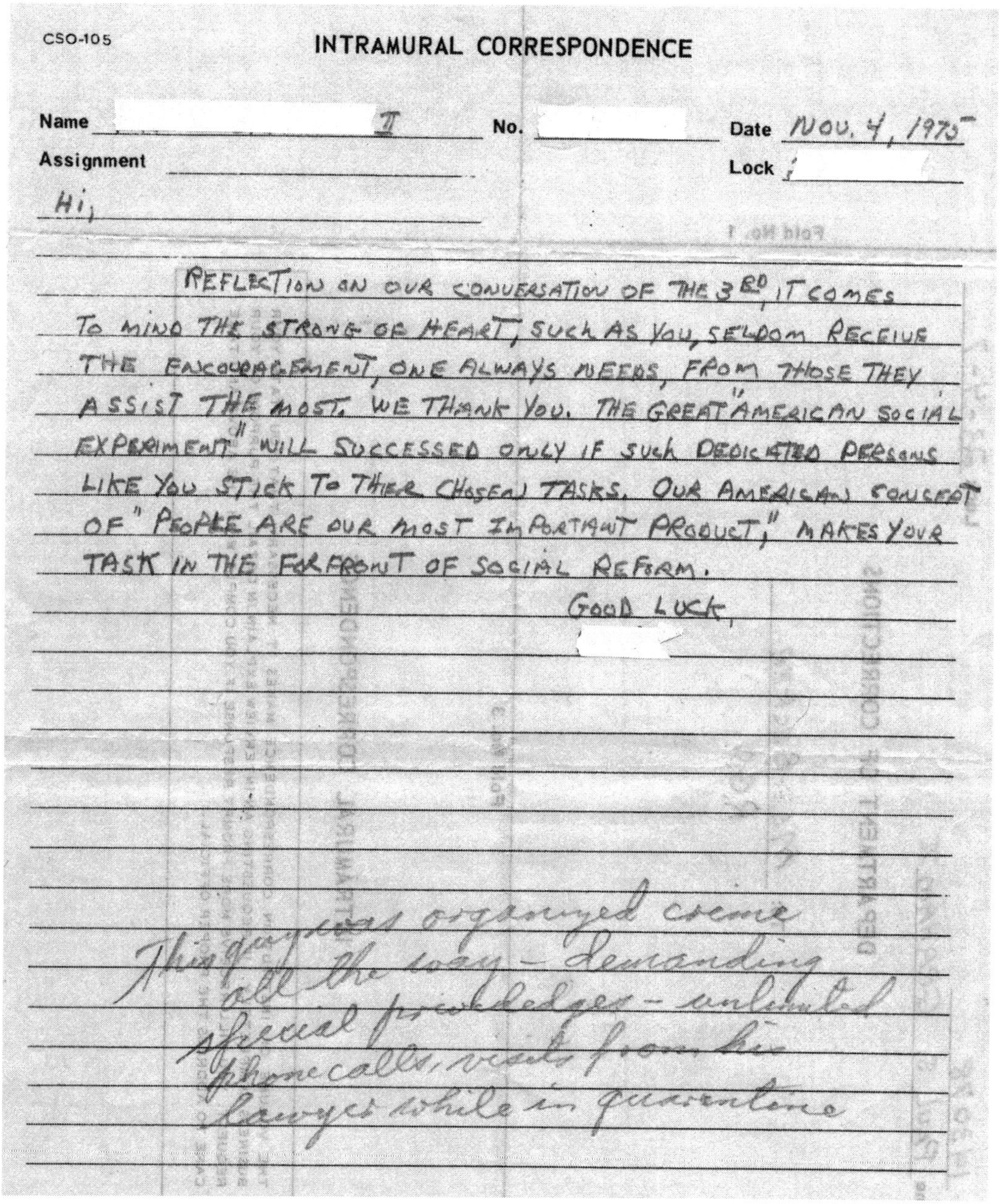

CSO-105   **INTRAMURAL CORRESPONDENCE**

Name _____ ℐ   No. _____   Date *Nov. 4, 1975*

Assignment _____   Lock ; _____

Hi, _____

REFLECTION ON OUR CONVERSATION OF THE 3ᴿᴰ, IT COMES
TO MIND THE STRONG OF HEART, SUCH AS YOU, SELDOM RECEIVE
THE ENCOURAGEMENT, ONE ALWAYS NEEDS, FROM THOSE THEY
ASSIST THE MOST. WE THANK YOU. THE GREAT "AMERICAN SOCIAL
EXPERIMENT" WILL SUCCESSED ONLY IF SUCH DEDICATED PERSONS
LIKE YOU STICK TO THIER CHOSEN TASKS. OUR AMERICAN CONCEPT
OF "PEOPLE ARE OUR MOST IMPORTANT PRODUCT," MAKES YOUR
TASK IN THE FORFRONT OF SOCIAL REFORM.

                GOOD LUCK,

*This guy was organized crome
all the way — Demanding
special prowledges — unlimited
phone calls, visits from his
lawyer while in quarentine*

Figure 9 - Some of the men interviewed seemed to appreciate our efforts — or was it manipulation?!

59

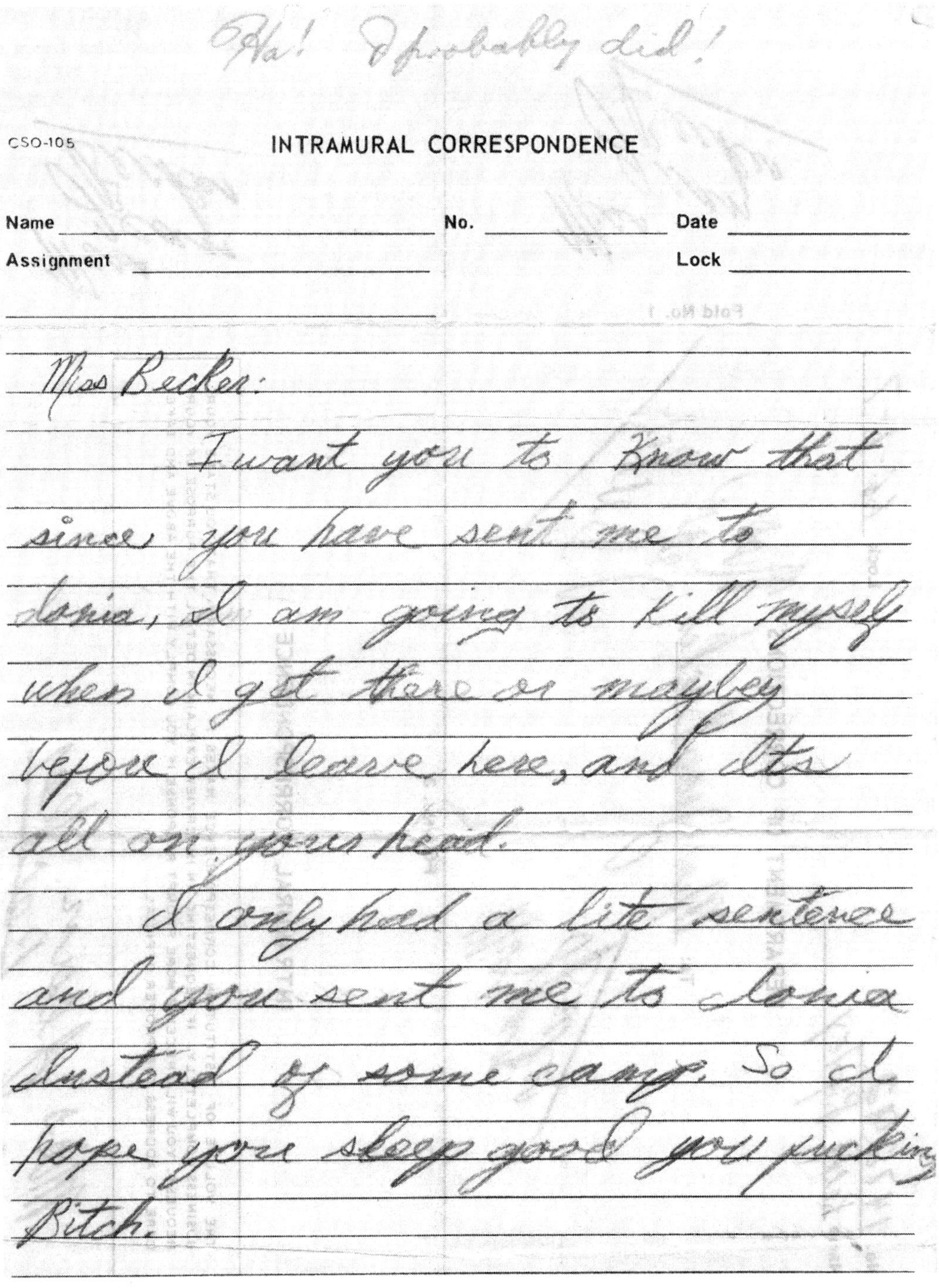

Ha! I probably did!

CSO-105

INTRAMURAL CORRESPONDENCE

Name _____ No. _____ Date _____

Assignment _____   Lock _____

_____

Miss Becker:

I want you to know that since you have sent me to Iowa, I am going to kill myself when I get there or maybe before I leave here, and Its all on your head.

I only had a lite sentence and you sent me to Iowa Instead of some camp. So I hope you sleep good you fucking Bitch.

Figure 10 - Then on the other hand....!!

60

ask if he could get sleeping pills. The black kid I saw a few days ago, who related to me as though I was his mother, stopped in unannounced, today--- to show me pictures of his family! That gave me a good feeling. He said I was the first person who "treat him right" since he's been inside. I also ran into psychotic Joe today and asked him if he is getting his medicine OK, and he smiled and thanked me because yes, he finally is.

Oh my, the gals in the typing pool told me today that my reports are the best, and they wish all the psychologists were women! They are a nice bunch. Did I mention, though, that the records office is strictly guarded by a martinet named Mabel, who evidently has been in charge there forever, and who seems to expect that the files we are assigned to pick up there will somehow be lost or desecrated by all us uncaring psychologists! Nary a smile can be coaxed from her. No way, no how.

Paul stopped in today to take me to lunch, and we had a bit of a therapy session. This time it was about his concerns. The food was terrible, as usual. The meat is full of grizzle, the ashes from the server's cigarettes are apt to land somewhere on our trays, and I suspect viewing the lack of sanitation in the kitchen would make us nauseous!

Thursday, Nov. 13th

I was so busy today that I forgot to pick up my first paycheck! And my new watch lost time, so I almost didn't get out by the witching hour. But that is the end of the day, not the beginning.

I saw some interesting cases today--- a run of manics, for some reason. I let Lou take my last man, as I was running late. He had come down to my office to talk about tomorrow, when I'm to sit in with him for a reduced custody hearing.

The young retarded boy stopped in today to tell me they hadn't moved him to base, and he's being hassled worse! He was shaking. I went to the control desk again, very angry, and *this time* they complied with what I asked. Warren (a nice officer) said he had talked with the kid every day, and I guess he figured that was enough. I wonder how any of the officers would like to spend the night on fourth gallery--- it's clear even to a "fish" like me, what often goes on up there.

I also had a religious convert, Gil, stop in to get support for holding services that he hopes to get going for the residents. He seems like a very sincere guy, but I did worry afterwards about the few things I told him when we shared some experiences. Doing this with a resident is not a good idea, generally.

I lost some of Paul's reports the other night when I left in such a hurry. I guess they were put in the wrong basket. Oh me! I ate with Dr. C. and Houseworth.

Friday, Nov. 14th

This was my first day to sit in with Classification! It was really a rest from the stress of cases, and it was fun to be with Steve Ribby and learn from him. I'd never had a chance to get to know him before, because he was on vacation when I started. Anyway, the room up there is more or less above my office, a gallery up--- and is small and hot with a fan to make it bearable, and is glassed in. Steve has a button he presses each time he wants to see a new man, and he goes so fast, it makes your head swim! But he always has a joke or some pleasantry, to try and put the man at ease as he delivers the fateful message of where in the system the man will do his time. All I was required to do was to put the results down. The young rapist I'd seen was one of the men, and completely different than when I saw him. He was sullen and defiant, this time. Steve says my reports are helpful. The morning went fast. Houseworth took over for a while and it went much more slowly, as he spent time deliberating. The emphasis is on camp placement, apparently. I'm careful when I recommend camp, because in spite of nice surroundings and reduced custody level, they have less in programs and there is less protection there from predators.

At noon, Steve and Houseworth asked me to go out with them and Earl Grier for lunch. I rode with Don and had a nice conversation. He thinks (rightly) that I enjoy being feminine--- (are we getting pretty personal, here?) After the meal, the guys played "odd man out" to see who would pay. I was too broke to play, but then I found they meant to pay mine! Earl was odd man. I'll try and pay him for it later.

This afternoon I was with Lou Hosner doing reduced custody cases, over in SPSM proper in a small room near the rotunda. It's fascinating to watch him, and the cases were interesting, too. One was a huge black man who has medical problems. He thanked us profusely, calling us "whites who really care about an ugly old black man." After we'd seen three or four and were done for the afternoon, we went upstairs for coffee and talked awhile. Lou told me of threats he's faced, and how he's backed antagonists down--- but he told me I'd be especially vulnerable, and if I have to put my name on a controversial report that will make someone a potential enemy, to let him sign it for me. He's sincere, I'm sure, and I appreciate his offer, but I hope I never feel so fearful that I have to take him up on it. He also gave me one of his little "brain teasers" and I failed utterly! He probably has me pegged as a retard now!

Monday, Nov. 17th

I was on classification again today, but with Ronald. It was much different than with Steve. No humor, and the men were more sullen. But I do like Ronald, too. We saw 28 this morning and were late for lunch, so I went over to the SPSM waiting room and learned to use the microwave oven to heat a hamburger. This afternoon, I saw three men but felt I didn't do well, that the reports were too trite and that I didn't get at the dynamics, and so on.

Oh, the grandson of a personal friend stopped me in the block. He's a resident, and in all kinds of trouble. I invited him to come down to my office for a talk sometime. It's about all I can do. Four or five people stopped by to ask for help of one kind or another today. They just open the door and walk in, generally, though some do knock. I'm getting used to knowing what I can and cannot do for them.

The highlight of the day, though---! I forgot to mention that last Friday, Cowboy, one of the cadre who, they say, runs the block as much as custody does, (he's a D or E man!) poked his head into my doorway and asked, "Ms. Becker, how'd you like a rug?" I said, "Oh Cowboy, wherever would you get a *rug*?" (I know that getting even an unbroken desk is quite a feat around here!) He said, "Never you mind, if you want one, Cowboy will get it." And he shut the door. I didn't think much about it afterward, but today when I arrived, I opened my door, and there, neatly installed, was a green shag rug!! I guess I will have to continue to wonder where it came from, because Cowboy won't tell me! I guess I hadn't mentioned Cowboy before. He's cadre like the clerks, apparently, but with different tasks, one of which seems to be taking care of us psychs! So now, my office is distinguished by having a rug underfoot, however worn and humble it may be!

I was very unhappy with the counselor's report on the young, retarded man I was so concerned about. He failed to mention any of the important aspects of the case, and recommended camp as placement. I'm glad I was at Classification when this boy's name came up--- Ronald assigned him to MTU (the Michigan Training Unit) where he will be in a medium security institution where he won't be quite as vulnerable to predators as he would be at camp.

I barely finished by 4:15. It was a full day, as usual.

Tuesday, Nov. 18th

Today the new man, Edward Benjamin, was with me. He's taken Bob's office, so is a neighbor. Bob now has a corner office, which is larger and, I believe, even has a window! Bob has been here all of 9 months longer than I have, and is being rewarded. Edward has quite a few qualms about working here, mostly having to do with the setting. He says his wife is "agin it!" We saw three interesting cases, but one went "out of it" (psychotic) before our eyes, and was so hostile and threatening, we were thankful when he left peacefully. I never did get the third report dictated, due to going up to eat early. Bob and I ate together and Ethan joined us.

Then we all had to attend staff training. It was very disorganized, which I have come to expect. They couldn't settle on a meeting place, so we went first to a room in the prison proper, then back to our own testing room in the building in Seven Block. As usual, lots of "discussion" and hard feelings were obvious. The amount of new duties heaped on us was horrendous! I think everyone is nervous about starting work tomorrow, when we will be responsible for everything the counselors did, such as conducting the initial interview with each new resident, and gathering much of the pertinent information from the man's files that is needed for classification.

We heard criticism, too, from George Bowman about sending men to Top Six inappropriately. That was aimed at me, I imagine!

Today was changeover day when we will be responsible for everything the counselors did. I got off to a slow start, due to the dictation I should have done yesterday morning, some phone calls, and worry about locating a missing file. Actually, there's a bit more work with the new system, but it does make sense, and since I usually pay close attention to relevant information in the files anyway, it's not too different for me.

I finished one and a half cases by lunch time. I called around for an escort, but didn't locate anyone, so I went through the bubble and into the marvelous fresh air! I asked for change at the store, and bought myself a bacon-beef cheeseburger from the machines. Then I went downstairs and sat with Tyrone Marshall again, and we had a nice conversation. He says the resident who gave me a rug yesterday, Cowboy, is a permanent fixture (doing life on the installment plan!), and he followed this with a few less complimentary comments. I suspect there is some sort of a past history, here, but I didn't ask further. Did I mention that Cowboy always wears a blue knitted cap with a bright red tassel on top? No mistaking him for anyone else in the block, ever! I do appreciate my "new" rug.

I slowed down a bit in the afternoon, but luckily, I couldn't see one of my men because he was in the infirmary. They gave him to Lou to do instead, as it's a long way across the yard to get out there. Because of that, I had lots of time. I went out of my office for a while, and talked with Gil, the resident who has been going around signing people up for Bible study, He was being helped by a young man I interviewed *weeks ago* so I asked him if he knew why he was still here, and he said someone else had gone to see the counselor and used his name.(?) The last I'd heard from him was the other day when he yelled at me from across the gallery, "I'm still *here!*"

I don't seem to be having more trouble with the new system than anyone else, which is a consolation. I probably wasn't that used to the old system yet, when the counselors sorted out some of the information for us on the men we are to see. Maybe it was kind of a duplication of duties, after all.

Ronald wrote a note on my first parole evaluation, that it was an excellent report! I feel good.

I saw a boy today who had never known love from anyone until adulthood. He had lived with a mentally ill mother. It was so sad.

Don dropped in again today and said I looked "charming!" The whistlers are at it again—now from behind my ventilating fan, which opens to the catwalk. Oh well. An officer told me today that his one pleasant duty was letting me in and out of the ramp!! The well-meant blarney really does make working here a bit nicer! I wish all the officers were that pleasant. And lastly, Lou showed me his VW lined in leopard skin!

Thursday, Nov. 20th

This was a bad day. I felt sick to my stomach to start with. Then I was given a list of things I'd done wrong on the new reports--- from the typing pool! No, not all the comments were bad, as Shirley says they have been discussing me--- how much they all like me! Anyway, Edward didn't have anyone to sit in with today, so I took him up to Classification with me, and we both got an earful!! Steve was in a bad mood today, and spoke as though everything I do is wrong, somehow, recommendation-wise. So he totally disregarded my recommendations in several cases that I'd felt were important. One man I'd advised to get into psychotherapy, but Steve sent him to *camp*. Luckily, the man dropped into my office later, and I told him about contacting Community Mental Health after he's released. Anyway, Houseworth also came in and made another correction on the new format for "case summary." There is another staff meeting tomorrow.

I ate with Edward and Jimmy. It looks as though Jimmy and I are lowest on the totem pole, status-wise. Edward hired in as a 12, as he has a Ph.D.--- and I'm only an 08 trainee!

This afternoon, I saw one man, then went over to GOS (main office) to pick up files on men I had to review for reduced custody and parole evaluations, as was requested by Paul. But I felt very frustrated, rubber-stamping his reports without having seen the men, as I am not quite confident that I know how to tell yet what should be recommended--- I read the files and Paul's reports and initialed all nine, but with some misgivings. It's quite a responsibility. Also, it was raining, and a resident called me a bitch--- And the office is so dirty I feel grimy all over. And the roaches--- They say there was a stabbing, and two escapes last night. I feel really down on the whole system and my part in it, right now. I try very hard to take into account all the information I read in the files, then I interpret the tests, and add to all that my impressions from the interview, in order to recommend the most appropriate placement for each man I see. What good does it do if I turn out the best report in the world and no one pays any attention??

Friday, Nov. 21st

I hope I didn't jeopardize my job today. It began in the car this morning, when I felt teary after telling Ronald that my morale is at an all-time low—due to yesterday, and continuing conflict over Ribby's role as Classification Officer, versus ours as psychologists. When we got to the cell block, I walked in with Ronald, and he invited me over (out to his office in the yard) since he wanted to give me the word on my one-month rating, anyway. So I did go out, and promptly went on a brief crying jag. I really hadn't realized how hard it had all hit me. Ronald suggested I might feel better about what I'm doing if I could handle a therapy group. This is true, but is a scary thought, too! Ronald is great to talk with, and it helped.

I went back to my office and got through the morning, then had lunch with Paul and Edward. Paul mentioned that he'd felt I was upset in the car this morning and wanted to help, but was uncertain what to do, with Ronald there. So he came in my office and we talked for about twenty minutes. He and Ronald are my good friends, and I started crying again for no good reason. Talking *did* help. Don had stopped in this morning too, and I mentioned my frustration and that I'd seen Ronald, and he told me I should try to be patient, since three years ago, Lou was the *only* psychologist in Seven Block, and now we are hiring more all the time, and so on. He and Ronald both told me that I'm one of those they depend on the most.

Then, of all things, Steve Ribby called and asked me to come up to his office! I thought maybe Ronald had told him I was upset, and why, but no--- for when I didn't get up there right away, Steve came storming down to tell me everything that was wrong with my reports since Tuesday! I cannot believe I messed them up *that* much. I thought later that I should have asked him how *he* gets them from the typists before I do! There could be typing pool errors, which I am always to have a chance to correct *before* they are distributed!

At 2:45 we had a staff meeting in the testing room. Don led it, and there were hassles over every point, but it did help clarify a lot of the new procedures. Shirley, one of our typists, was there. She'd been escorted into the block, as she's deathly afraid to be in here. She's very likeable and I talked with her later. She was really put off by the squabbling, and the language some of the staff use so freely upset her too, and she told them so! Maybe I should be bothered by it also, but I'm not, really, because it is so common in here. I hardly ever use profanity, however, and don't expect to, not because I'm a prude, but because it just isn't "me," and I don't plan to change because of my surroundings.

Oh yes, I hear I'm to get some sort of "assertiveness training" before long from Ribby and Frank Griffith. Frank has a clinical social worker degree, as does Jimmy, but they are doing the same work as the psychologists.

Monday, Nov. 24th

I'm back at it, as usual, past the mops this morning and the new men gawking. This was a busy morning. I seem to be interrupted every few seconds, and this makes dictating a report pretty hard. Otherwise, I am mostly holding my own on the number of men I see. It's been a month since I started, and I feel like an old hand already. (Except for last Friday, of course, which I hope was an aberration!) I do try to treat each resident I interview as an individual, as much as possible. I will admit, though, that after interviewing as many as 70 or more men in the past month, it becomes difficult to recall any particular one later, unless there is something outstanding about him or his case.

I was scheduled to relieve Earl Grier in his office at 11:45 while he has lunch, and I had barely enough time to get mine before that. The guards in the subhall are getting used to me. Once in a while, though, they keep us from crossing the crosswalk from the yards until there is less traffic, as it is a very busy intersection. The food was REALLY terrible in the OD today--- turkey tetrazzini. It tasted rancid and we didn't eat the meat as a safety precaution. The inmates in the "Big Top" dining room just below the OD get the same food, which I figure just might be a part of their punishment! The raisin bread tasted good, though. Todd Miller, Edward and Paul were there, a nice bunch. Todd is in charge of all the testing that is done on newly arriving inmates.

Relieving Earl Grier wasn't bad, it just meant taking a few phone calls and sitting and talking with people as they came in to see him. But it did put me behind, and I never did catch up. Luckily, Edward didn't have a case this afternoon, so he took one of mine.

I had another upset with Steve. Somehow, he manages to make me feel like a child! But he assures me he is willing to help me when I need it. My training in assertiveness is to be Dec. 1 through 4. Will it help me to stand up to Steve, I wonder?

Some of my cases were repeaters today. They are much harder, as there is so much more paper to go through, since we have to be familiar with everything pertinent in all the old files, as well as the PSI's (pre-sentence investigations) from the current case, and of course, all the testing results. Also, we no longer have counselors' reports, (one of the recent changes), which means it takes us a lot longer in order to be sure we haven't missed something important.

A resident (porter) came in and cleaned my office this afternoon. He seemed OK. I do suspect that the old pros in that group are trying to "take me in" a bit, but I hope not. For example, one of the cadre clerks told me today that I look better with my hair this new way. They seem like nice young men, though. I often wonder what they did that sent them here. I heard that one clerk was charged with taking $500 from a resident for supposedly using his "influence" with the psychs as to his classification!

This was an unusual day (aren't they all??) I had to get up and get going at 5:45 this morning, as a lot of the white stuff, so common in the winter, fell last night and it is my day to drive. I did OK behind the wheel of my trusty old Dodge Demon, if I do say so myself, and we arrived just about on time. It was funny--- Ronald punched in just ahead of Paul and me, and was on time, and we were one minute late, and so had to wait until 4:30 to punch out after work!

I saw my first man OK, but when I called the second, no one answered. I assumed he was "skating" (not where he is supposed to be---a ticketable offense.) So I decided to finish up odds and ends, and then go to lunch. Edward came over and asked me to go with him, and he mentioned that staff meeting was coming up, which I'd forgotten. On the way through the subhall, he left me there in the hall while he stopped in the rest room. I felt really uneasy standing there. Some residents spoke, and seemed friendly, so no harm was done. One large black man came up and said to me with a laugh, "You know he's going against administrative security by doing that, don't you?" The meal was so bad in the OD that no one ate very much. There were big chunks of grizzle in anemic-looking gravy.

The staff meeting was better, though there was still a lot of friction. We discussed just how wide open to lawsuits we all are. It seems that when we make recommendations that the resident doesn't like, or misinterpret something in their files, or write an unfavorable report on them for the parole board, and so on, they sometime get litigious! When I got back to my office, I discovered I was supposed to relieve Earl Grier again--- and he'd given up waiting! I apologized later. There is so much to remember around here! I also discovered that the man I'd called for in the morning *was* present, and was still sitting there on the bench, waiting! I'd pronounced his name wrong when I'd called him. So, at that point, I went to the office and had all three men (two were afternoon cases) put on recall for another day, because I was scheduled for court. Actually, I only had to sit in, due to Houseworth's last minute decision, so the pressure was off. In court, we saw five cases in the classification room. One resident was extremely angry when told he was to be locked in Six Block for his own protection. It was a tense moment. Several residents had been beaten by gangs of black residents who apparently thought it good sport to prey on vulnerable "honkies". At one point, all the committee rushed out when it sounded like an emergency in the block, but it was a false alarm. Ty was there, and Officer Wyman and one other officer. But all was well. As we were finishing, Steve Ribby came in, and I stayed to talk with him. He was feeling fine today, and explained a lot to me that I didn't realize, about his responsibilities. I finally went back down to my office--- and lo and behold, the same man was there on the bench, *still* waiting to be seen! He says, "I'm still here!" I felt like two cents, as the expression goes, and decided to talk with him then and there, even though I knew I'd never have time to get the report dictated today--- and didn't.

Wednesday, Nov. 26th

Tomorrow is Thanksgiving. I guess they even have turkey in R&GC! Today was bedlam--- many new arrivals, the horrible banging while they test the bars, a general uproar in the population. It was grim and scary. I finished up yesterday's work and most of the morning's, before calling Paul about lunch. While I was waiting at Paul's door for him, I heard a group of residents coming my way. One whooped, "There's a *WOMAN* in here!" But then, no more comments were made and I saw why, when they came by. Cowboy was with them---hat with pom-pom and all---and he spoke and joked with me. Bless his heart---I sure was nervous for a few seconds! It's ever more clear to me that Cowboy and his crew intend to protect me, at least when I am in Seven Block, because, of course, they cannot follow me elsewhere in SPSM.

Paul and I went up to the Rose Room (OD) for lunch around 11:00. He also left me standing in the subhall momentarily, and when we got to the stairs, the guard there took him aside and requested that he not do it again. Poor Paul. I wish I didn't have to ask the guys to escort me all the time.

Anyway, I had to hurry through lunch, as I was to relieve Earl again. I walked back with Edward. While I was encamped in Earl's office, Steve Ribby came in and talked with me for a lot of the time I was there. Interesting--- but I wonder why? I do like him, but he's so changeable.

I saw two men with long records today. One had just finished a term at Leavenworth--- a narcotics dealer with a concurrent sentence, so he will be

71

leaving us. There was also a sad case, a black kid who got a ticket and appeared in court yesterday. He is mentally in the defective range (66), young, small, and he began to cry in my office. He had just been slapped around by predators. I called Frank, who said there's nothing that can be done. But I took him down to Control anyway, and politely asked my officer friend there if the boy could be toplocked (a secure cell lock) for his own safety. He said OK, as soon as possible, and sent the boy back to his house (cell). When I came back from lunch, several men were outside the boy's cell, harassing him verbally. I gave them the eye, and they left. However, the poor kid was still there when I left tonight. I told him to play it cool and I'll check on him on Friday. I just know I'll worry about the situation over Thanksgiving.

I also interviewed our friend's grandson today. Tonight I asked Steve what I should have done, and he said I should have disqualified myself! Oh dear. And Don brought in a gal my age, who may be offered a job here. She seemed OK. Edward and I both left *early* tonight---shhh! We both had our work done so went to the lunchroom for a coke.

Friday, Nov. 28th

A lot of the staff were off today, taking advantage of a long weekend. Dr. C. is seeing six men a day, now, as he's been here a few weeks longer than I have. I'm usually still on four. I saw a psychotic this morning and so did Edward, so we compared notes; his man was worse than mine. I was so busy today that I didn't even get to my mailbox, where we get notes (kites) from residents--- of all kinds! They are usually asking for something. I went to lunch with Edward, who wanted to stop at the men's room, but I dissuaded him by telling him of Paul's experience yesterday. I was supposed to relieve Earl again (jokes by Paul about that!) but got back from lunch at 11:45 to find Houseworth had been sitting in for me at Earl's office, and had left. So I got a head start on the afternoon. I almost always seem to use up every minute, anyway, so it's a good thing.

I saw a man with an IQ well over 120 this afternoon, a good-looking black who was a senior at Wayne state and also a *big time* narcotics dealer. He had no remorse at all. I had a hard time with that and couldn't find anything likeable about him. Edward says I was being "maternalistic"---ha! Anyway, I guess maybe

I was, because I recommended him for group counseling, hoping perhaps he'll see some of the sort of human wrecks he has helped to create, first hand. He didn't even need the money! Then on the way out tonight, I ran into our friend's grandson again, and didn't recognize him. I hope the men aren't all beginning to be indistinguishable to me. This wasn't a good way to end the day.

Monday, Dec. 1st

This was a blustery morning and I wore my new platform boots. They looked great, I think, and hopefully make me look a bit taller than 5' 2", but they pinched some by evening. I saw five men today, and barely finished, as usual. One had knifed a girl in the back and set fire to a neighbor's house--- and was sentenced to only nine months!! I was called upstairs in the middle of the morning to screen for a parole evaluation--- on Cowboy! I gave my opinion that since it was a screening and not the evaluation itself, and since the Superintendent, Ty, etc., wrote letters for him, he should get the chance (he had broken up some trouble on the block) but Jimmy and Steve both disagreed. Two prevail against one. Poor Cowboy.

There was a lot of noise today and apparently some trouble, as James popped in to see if I was all right. And we have a new procedure now, which is a pain. We must walk the files up to the bubble at noon as well as at night. I protest! I may make a point of it at staff meeting tomorrow.

I also saw one boy who is supposed to be a psychiatric case, but all I saw was a nervous sociopath. Well--- I could be wrong, as I'm not infallible. But I have learned that my instincts are pretty accurate, most of the time. Oh, I also heard that our friend's grandson is in trouble again. They found him with a syringe. I wonder if his "cold" the other day really was a "cold?" I'm surely disappointed in him, and at the moment, I feel quite blue about the whole place.

Tuesday, Dec. 2nd

Snow and slippery roads again, but it was Paul's day to drive. This morning I saw a multiple sex offender. After reading the file, I expected the worst. He has a low IQ, is sadistic, hates women, and has *seven* arrests for rape.

STATE OF MICHIGAN

DEPARTMENT OF CORRECTIONS

RECEPTION AND GUIDANCE CENTER RECOMMENDATION

NAME	NUMBER	AGE	STA-TUS	READING: MATH:	A.G.E.	TERMS	PLACE-MENT	DATE
		30	F		Below 4.0	2y5m-4	J	8-2-76

RECOMMENDATION:	CLOSE		TRANSFERRED

This committee once again makes reference to the "MANAGEMENT" section of this case. It has been recommended that Mr. _____ be sent for an evaluation to the Clinical Services Unit. For further references to these statements, please refer to the "MANAGEMENT" section.

MANAGEMENT: SPSM-CLOSE is definitely recommended for Mr. _____ who demonstrated a break-down of integrated thinking during the interview. He seems to be maintaining himself at present in general population, but his reality contact is variable and if his disorganization continues, he should be sent for an evaluation to the Clinical Services Unit. This man has shown his assaultive behavior against family members and has been convicted of a sex offense against his own daughter. He has spent time in state hospitals but a psychiatric report is not presently available. There do not seem to be pending charges and there is no evidence of any escapes on his record.

EDUCATION: NO RECOMMENDATION is made for Mr. _____ whose present disorganization seems to be adversely affecting his testing. The Revised Beta Examination indicates that he is performing in the mentally defective range. His academic skills are rated as below fourth grade level. However, it would not be beneficial to coerce Mr. _____ into attendance in the SCHOOL PROGRAM at the present time.

JOB READINESS: ROUTINE WORK ASSIGNMENT might prove helpful for Mr. _____ who tends to withdraw from reality and to his own fantasy world when left to his own devices. At the time of the instant offense he was unemployed and actually had little in the way of a work record in the community.

SUBSTANCE ABUSE: NO RECOMMENDATION is made for Mr. _____ who drinks but does not use drugs. Mr. _____ does not believe that he has a drinking problem, and with his low AGE would not be suitable for a SUBSTANCE ABUSE PROGRAM.

PHYSICAL HEALTH: NO RECOMMENDATION is made for Mr. _____ at this time. His medical clearance is not yet in the file.

TRANSFER AS INDICATED ABOVE IS HEREBY ORDERED

DIRECTOR OF CLASSIFICATION	DATE	DEPUTY DIRECTOR IN CHARGE OF BUREAU OF CORRECTIONAL FACILITIES
DMS/sdd		

STATUS: F-FIRST TERM. C-FIRST TERM-CONC. SENT. R-REPEATER. N-PVNS, V-TECH. VIOL., E-ESCAPE SENT., L-LIFERS-LONG SENT., M-MURDER 1ST

PLACEMENT: J-SPSM, W-CAMPS, M-MARQUETTE, I-REFORMATORY, T-TRAINING UNIT C-CASSIDY LAKE, D-DHC, K-MUSKEGON Q-MIPC

CRO- 101   R&GC — RECOMMENDATION

CLINICAL IMPRESSIONS: When Mr.   was called to the interview, he was sleeping on the bench and did not respond. He indicated immediately that he intends to sleep a great deal and stated that he does daydream alot. As the interview progressed, his verbalizations became more and more confused and he appeared incapable of responding coherently to the questions asked. He did let the interviewer know that he feels unfavorably toward psychologists who pry into his personal thoughts. For this reason, he was allowed to ventilate verbally for awhile and then was dismissed. He certainly demonstrated, in his verbalizations, considerable psychotic reorganization of experience but upon being told it was time to leave, responded appropriately. As stated under management, Mr.   evidently has demonstrated assaultive behavior towards his own family and has been convicted of an assaultive offense as well as a sex offense. This interviewer feels that he could manifest violent behavior if sufficiently frustrated or threatened.

TREATMENT OBJECTIVES: EVALUATION BY CLINICAL SERVICES UNIT will probably be in order for Mr.   Custodial staff has been alerted to be on the alert for any bizarre behavior and that a CSU evaluation may be in order.

                                        Joan Becker - Clinical Psychologist

7-29-76
JB/pjw
7-30-76

Orig:
  cc: Counselor
      Lansing Record Office (2)
      Institutional Main File
      Psych File

Figure 11 - Previous page and above – This is a sample of a "Transcase" which was dictated after a new resident was interviewed. Recommendation at the top was the Classification Committee's determination as to where the man would be sent.

But as I should have expected by now, he was putting his best foot forward when he was in my office. He gave the usual story of "wanting to go straight" (after having spent 15 of his almost 30 years behind bars!) What really got to me was that one rape in the past wasn't prosecuted, in part because the gal was a lesbian. Wow! Whose idea of justice was that?? And it looks as though things haven't changed that much. His sentence for the latest rape? 1 1/2 to 2 years (which actually means 9 months). I have to question whether the judge in the case belongs on the bench at all!

The next two cases I discovered I couldn't do, because I had the wrong files, so they were recalled and Edward and I went to lunch early. I still catch a glimpse of the man in six block watching for me, and he murmurs a greeting every day as I go by.

Staff meeting today was relatively calm, as Houseworth and Lou were not present. Lou stopped in my office later, and offered to let me sit in on his sex offender group sometime. This afternoon I only had two cases, so was done early, and Edward and I went over to the lunchroom for a cup of coffee. I no longer feel guilty about taking a bit of time off, as we are not allowed any coffee breaks during the day, obviously.

Wednesday, Dec. 3rd

They assigned me three men today. And I found out I goofed yesterday. I was supposed to pick up the missing folders and didn't. I was excused from seeing one man in the morning, as Lou had done him yesterday, but the work piled up in the afternoon, and one guy was a non-stop talker. I'm afraid I was extra hard on him, as he was a southern redneck-type who shot his black neighbor in a shoot-out. I also saw a 33 year old repeater this morning who'd just been given a new 35 to 50 year sentence. He was a mental defective, and angry. I could hardly wait to get him out of my office! I also saw a schizophrenic rapist. Great day! I ate downstairs with Edward today, because the menu in the OD features *liver!* No way! Jimmy was involved in a "shout-out" with someone on the gallery today.

The Superintendent asked me if I'd like to work at De Ho Co (women's prison outside Detroit), when I saw him in the bubble today. Ohmygosh!---without thinking, I said, "No thanks, I like men!"--- which is true, but is hardly the thing to say to the superintendent!

Thursday, Dec. 4th

I was given six files today, and started sputtering right away--- and to Don, of all people! He gave me the paternal bit and told me how, when I am more used to the job, I can keep up with the others! Grrrr. I should know when to keep still! As it happened, the clerks took one away in the morning, and Ethan took another in the afternoon. Nothing unusual, and I had plenty of time. I ate with Ethan this noon--- downstairs, because I couldn't find anyone to go to the OD with me. I actually started through Six Block by myself, but got cold feet and went out the ramp to the bubble instead. Then Ethan invited me to sit with him, Mr. Monroe, et al. from Top Six. That was unusual, as CSU staff and PSU staff are usually at odds, unfortunately.

I was supposed to be on classification today, but someone took me off at the last minute. I'm a little sorry they did. After work, Don walked with me and also mentioned De Ho Co, and would I like to go with him for a visit? I guess I acted uptight about it (I felt that way too!) and he assured me there is no plan to transfer me "right now"(?) There is *no* way I want to work at Detroit House of Corrections!! It would be a *very* long commute, and that place does not have a good reputation as a place to work. I have a splitting headache!

Friday, Dec. 5th

Another week is behind me. This was an interesting day. I saw three men this morning. One of them was toplocked, and had to be brought down by Officer Bishop. I almost didn't get the man back to Bishop, afterward---he went walking off by himself! I saw Cowboy, who looked at me soulfully--- poor guy. I called Lou at lunchtime. Then Houseworth joined us, and a group of us had fun walking to lunch together. This is the first time I've been propositioned at *noon* in a long time---ha! It is beautiful weather. Houseworth says the secretaries tell him my reports and Edward's are the best of any! And that he takes great stock in what they say.

This afternoon, I finished up the morning's work and then waited in my office, until time for the first of this week's group sessions for employees. Jimmy dashed in first, all upset. He received notice this morning that he's fired! A technical mix up, I'm sure. (I hope!) But he was pretty scared. I know it is rumored that the counselors, who are mostly social workers, are being replaced ASAP by psychologists, but most are being relocated, not fired. And although his degree is in social work, Jimmy does do the same work the rest of us psychs do.

I also put several men on call today, as they had written me wanting various favors, including medicines, etc. I can't usually help, but I listen. Oh, James M. (the new "Jim") sat in with me yesterday, listening. He confided to me that he has *no* clinical background, and has been given two weeks to make it up! Pretty well impossible, I'd say, since I studied for years and still never pretend to know it all! When I finally did get to group training this afternoon, it was "iffy" as to its usefulness. It looks as though it will be a lot like "empathy training." Lou made a fuss. Poor guy, he has been here so long, and doesn't dare change (but denies this!) Lillian, from word processing, is a member. Good! We spent most of the time filling out questionnaires, this session. Afterward, I went up for a cup of coffee with Lou, who's still defensive. Dr. C. came too. Anyway--- the staff dynamics around here are really interesting.

Monday, Dec. 8th

I was given three men to see by 11:00, but one was taken away, luckily. Of the two, one was very hostile. The other was a terrible manipulator, with one of the worst records I've seen. However, another man stopped back in today just to tell me where he's been sent, which made me feel very good. I went to lunch at 11:00 again, in order to be back and ready for group at 12:00.

The group was pure boredom. Four hours in which we were taught how to sit attentively. And not much else. We had frequent smoke breaks, too. I hope the rest of the week goes a bit better! I wonder whose bright idea it was to involve us in a "group therapy" type of staff training!

Tuesday, Dec. 9th

No one saw any men today. The computer broke down so there were no Psych reports. I spent part of the morning talking with Edward. I also received three kites asking for help, so I called the desk to have the men put on call. But no one came. At noon, the officer told me one was in segregation, one in top lock for some offense.

One of the first men I ever interviewed was back today. He came in just to talk, and told me he will soon be paroled. He gave me some nice compliments (he was a real manipulator before, so I guess I should deduce that he still is!) Edward saw Lansing's triple murderer today, said the guy was "a mess," crying and all. I don't imagine Edward did much to comfort him.

Group went better this afternoon. We met in the testing room in the block, and when we broke into half, one group went into Jimmy's office (the smokers). Our group consisted of Don, Officer Steadman, James M., Davis, me, and one of the leaders, of course. Don and I worked as a twosome. However, I told him off a bit, for constantly "analyzing" me privately. Later, when Edward and I talked after lunch, he commented on Don's interest in me and my ability to adjust to work in this setting.

Wednesday, Dec. 10th

Several interesting things happened today. I was called out of group to talk with a young gal who was interviewing for a job here. I felt she was a bit young and not quite ready, and said so to Don and Ronald. While she was in my office, a young resident who used to drop in, did so again, to see the girl, of course! Before he went out, he turned to her and asked her if she's going to work here, then asked how old she is? She said "twenty-four." He shook his head and said, "You're dead!" as he walked out! (??)

During group, custody started up a machine in the cell block to fix the locks, and whether the sound was reminiscent of a police car, or maybe a cop came in, but suddenly the whole place echoed with siren imitations. Funny! There were interesting things going on in group, with Don at the center.

I ate with Steve--- and he critiqued my reports--- and later I critiqued one of his placements! I had recommended "close" and he sent the man to camp. I'll bet sometime in the future, the man's behavior will prove that I was right!

Today Paul brought several pictures of his girl and his family to show to me and Ronald. It was nice of him.

I didn't quite finish my three morning men, so kept dashing back to my office during smoke breaks from the group. But--- as I was coming back from lunch through Six Block at noon, I just casually glanced across and there was a man stark naked in the shower--- and he was petrified when he saw me! I pretended not to have seen, and wished I really hadn't. Farther on, they were sweeping up glass and they warned me to be careful and not get hurt. Edward asked why no one cares if *he* gets hurt!

I saw one "bad actor" from Marquette, weighing 190 pounds and with a low IQ, and he was sitting there with muscles rippling, in a red undershirt. Almost everything he said was a lie. He had been caught with heroin in his jockstrap!

The group went OK, except that I floundered when I was to help Bob with his feelings about the Clinical Unit's criticisms. I was just too sensitive about it myself! I think (hope) I redeemed myself later. The porters interrupted group to ask me if I'd like a mirror in my office! Mark and Cowboy installed it and cleaned it very carefully. I guess Cowboy doesn't resent the turning down of his parole screening too badly. Oh yes--- James M's last day was today. There really wasn't much I could do to help him. He's taken another job. It seems odd that he got a job here at all, without training or a clinical degree. They must be desperate for clinicians.

Edward and I have had several talks. Our philosophies do not agree--- he is all for punishment and doesn't feel it's his job to relate with residents. He really dislikes them.

I challenged Steve once again on a classification. He had sent another guy to camp when I had recommended "close". The man had a really bad record all around. What earthly good does it do for me to exercise my skills and make the decisions that are demanded, if Steve can overturn them so easily? Some changes need to be made! Or have I expounded on this enough, before??

Kid on probation– robbery armed., 5 to 10. Had a homosexual relationship with his step-brother who is female appearing, but with a beard. He was kept by force, beaten, escaped but violated probation. His girlfriend is pregnant, and fears her lover will hurt her.

A married man, member of a motorcycle gang. He went to his girlfriend's house after a fight in a bar with a man, beat her and strangled her to death. Her five year old daughter hears screams, comes downstairs. The man beats and strangles the child until she is unconscious. Got natural life. He denies the offense, says the motorcycle gang is threatening his life as well as his wife and child.

A retarded boy from the upper peninsula. He was an abused child and left home after being severely beaten by his stepmother. He was living in a car, no food, and couldn't get welfare, so broke into some businesses. He is half scared to death, evidently has been pressed for sex by other residents, but couldn't talk to me about it. He had tears in his eyes and was shaking.

An old junkie-- well, he looked old, age 49. He has two teeth (one on each side) and needs glasses. He's been locked up most of his life. He was out just a couple of months and got hooked again. He did B & Es for money for heroin. But he blames everyone else.

A wild kid, this is his second time here. He discharged from parole last time and got a special, at that. Settled in a small town (his mistake!) and got arrested for being drunk, and marijuana charges, but no felony offense. He finally got charged for advising a girlfriend to keep still when a witness at a trial of someone else, and to take the fifth ammendment. They don't like him in that little town!

An epilectic. He broke into his girlfriend's house, had forcible sex with her 12 year old son. He denies the offense, in spite of many witnesses. Has only one month left to serve.

Monday, Dec. 15th

Today seemed rather bad, even for a Monday! I only got two files this morning, but they were both inches thick (as is the case with repeat offenders, who have long records, of course). I had just started reading one (and saw it would be bad) when I received word that I was to be on classification with

Ronald. I like working with Ronald, but it goes slowly. We didn't finish until 12:30. It worked out well, though, because he classified some of the men that I had interviewed, and agreed with my decisions on placement. It gave me a good feeling. Maybe the difference is that Steve is "Custody," and Ronald and I are "Treatment," with different objectives.

Anyway, I mentioned that I had a scary case coming up, and Ronald said he, or someone else, should be with me. So since I knew Ronald was busy, I asked Jimmy, who I bumped into on his way back from lunch. He offered me a life-saver, and said we would talk after I ate. I was starved by then. I'd missed lunch at the OD so I went out through the bubble and bought myself a hamburger in the lunchroom, and ate alone. Monroe, at the next table, didn't speak, and neither did I. Too bad--- it's PSU vs. CSU, and it's those hard feelings again.

I felt better when I got back to the block, and told Jimmy I was OK about seeing the man myself. Then I went into my office and promptly got cold feet again. By then, Jimmy had called Edward and told him to listen through the wall for any trouble, so Edward called to ask me if he should come over and sit in, and I gratefully accepted. So we saw the man together. He'd been hospitalized and/or incarcerated for over twenty years. He had killed his eighty-eight year old grandmother, first by knocking her head on the floor--- the report spoke of blood all over two rooms. He's back now from Mental Health for slitting the throat of his girlfriend, who was another patient. She lived, because he missed the jugular vein. In the meantime, he murdered another inmate or two. The forensic center report advised, "This man is as dangerous as any you'll ever see." So Edward and I were both pretty scared, and I only kept the man in my office for about five minutes. He looked weird, but was in touch with reality, at the moment, anyway. The guys asked Edward later what he'd have done if the man had pulled a razor on me, and Edward said, "I'd have run like hell--- to get help!!"

Anyway, the blues have hit us. We are all feeling it--- in large part because Earl Grier's desk clerk, Mark, who I must have mentioned, has been ticketed for a major misconduct. But for me, it's worse. I found out the last thing in the day, from the officer (guards are now addressed as "officers") who let us out of the ramp, that I'm to be the "advocate" for another inmate involved in the same case tomorrow! Plus, I was asked today if I'd also represent a second man, who had disobeyed an order. I was so busy, I didn't get to see the second man's witnesses at all, and I dread to think of tomorrow in Seven Block court!

Tall, blonde, ponytailed porter Hal stopped in today to tell me he's been dreaming about the gal I had in the office the other day--- and then he began flirting with me! Very inappropriate, and I wonder about him. Later, Jimmy, who is also to be an advocate in court tomorrow, told me that Hal can tell us who else is involved in the case being heard tomorrow, and may have other information I should know about. The block grapevine apparently works very well indeed!

Paul talked about one of his cases on the way home tonight. The guy had a sex orgy with a 15 year old, while both were on drugs. She overdosed and died. He'd been living with the girl's mother, who was a prostitute, and was scared to tell her, so he cut the girl's body up into five pieces and put them in plastic bags! Marvelous way to end the day!

Tuesday, Dec. 16th

This was another bad one--- I was assigned five men, and I *knew* I couldn't cope with them, and court too. So--- Lou took one off my hands right away (he apparently does this for anyone on the staff!) And then I conferred with Jimmy about the case, and began getting facts together on my own (like in a detective novel, but this is for *real*.) I interviewed Officer Sanders, Lt. Miller, and Hal, in person, and Sgt. Prentis by phone. I found out that my client, Dennis (a cadre clerk), supposedly borrowed Mark's coat when he went out of Seven Block to go to the store. (Cadre are inmates, but are not quarantined and are allowed to leave the block.) As he came back in, Officer Sanders frisked him, found Mark's scrip (used as cash in here) and ID in the jacket, along with Parsons' scrip as well. Dennis, who is worried about being charged with stealing Parsons' scrip, has said he was holding it for still another man, who is now locked in Five Block. Hal told me he saw someone steal it from Parsons' house (cell) and that he'd testify to that if he could be "safe". So I promised that I, personally, would not tell anyone but Jimmy, who is to represent Mark. So--- Jimmy came to my office and we talked--- in private, we thought, until Hal himself said "Hi" through my ventilation hole from outside on the catwalk! Privacy around here is a farce!

After that, I interviewed one man and did that report, but gave my other case to Lou. Then I went to lunch with Jimmy and Edward. Jimmy is all upset about the case (me too) because we both like Mark. Then, of all days, today was staff meeting. There wasn't much of import, but attending slowed me down some more.

Court was held at 12:30 in Ribby's office. Everyone had to wait, so I sat on the bench between Dennis and another man, and also saw Parsons and Mark--- and Cowboy, there! The officers didn't like my speaking with the men, and their hostility was apparent immediately. Mark and Jimmy went in first. When they came out, it was unsettled, but Jimmy indicated Ty was very hostile, watch out! And he was right--- Ty and Prentis Sturdevant and Officer Elliottson, especially Elliottson. They'd decided my man was guilty before he came in, or so it seems, and wouldn't even hear Hal's story (a "fish" has no weight). Finally, they were about to find my man, Dennis, guilty of possession of someone else's scrip and going to the store for someone else, when they realized the second count would also involve Mark. So--- they backed down and found Dennis guilty on just one count. Then we had to sweat out Parsons' verdict (not guilty, but barely!) Mark came over to the bench where I was sitting to tell me not to feel badly, whichever way it went, which was nice of him. Anyway, I did manage to get my second man off (and *he* was probably guilty!) but quoted my interview with Lt. Miller to do it, and Prentis--- calling attention to the confusion over who was a "state man" and who wasn't, and that the ticket was made out by Miller, not Griffith, and so on. I hope I didn't misrepresent in any way. I really didn't mean to. Anyhow, I felt good that Mark got off. I hope I never have to serve as an advocate at court again!

At that point, I was still assigned to see two more men in the afternoon. Edward volunteered to take one, but the man wasn't on the bench waiting, and I wondered if *he* was the actual scrip stealer?? An officer came in to see me, and wanted information on anything I knew about who that really was! I gave him the man's number that I'd received from Hal, but I didn't involve Hal. And I still had to finish up Parole Evaluations before leaving. Then, just to finish off a terrible day--- Jimmy told me in the lunchroom after work and in confidence, that he'd *heard* Mark ask Dennis to go to the store for him! In here, it's best not to trust *anyone!*

But wait, there's more! After I got home, I realized I'd forgotten something--- that the clerk had come in this morning around 10:00 and said Mr. Hosner (Lou) had decided to relieve me of seeing another man, so I'd said "Great," and had handed him the file to give to Lou. I just realized when I got home what I had done. I'd given a resident another man's file! I could get fired!! Or cause some resident a lot of trouble. Now I've got to pray that Lou *had* sent him, and that it wasn't the resident's scheme to get information he shouldn't have. Well, it was a nice (sort of) job, while it lasted!

Wednesday, Dec. 17th

This was another grim day. I had an emergency, Dolman, sitting on my doorstep at 8:00 A.M., demanding that I help him. So I went back through the ramp to the bubble to get his file. But even after reading it, I still couldn't decide if he is really "flakey" or just wants an easy way to do time. Later, Don came in and advised me not to send him to Top Six. So I tried to have him put on call for me in the afternoon, but Dan, our clerk, said scheduling him for tomorrow morning would be better, so I quit worrying about Mr. Dolman for the day.

I hadn't quite finished my second man's report when Jimmy and Edward came to pick me up for lunch. On the way through the bubble, they and Earl Grier began kidding me about my age (I've been around a bit longer than most of that group!) Then I guess they began worrying about it, because they asked if they had offended me, and explained that good-natured insults are a way of dissipating tension. So I told them that I wouldn't feel accepted if I *didn't* get kidded, but that I'm just not very good at handing it back!

Don got under my skin with his backhanded compliments again--- that "someday" I should be a real asset to the group!

In the afternoon, Jimmy came in, as angry as the proverbial wet hen. Hal Claymore has been relieved of his job as porter by Ty (Hal says) because he was to be my witness at Dennis' trial yesterday. That upset me, too, so I called Don to ask if I could talk with him, and was given a "yes." I went out to his office in the yard and told him the story. At first he preached again but then he called Officer Riley who verified what I had said. So Don called the Superintendent, who promptly blew up at Don for making a fuss about "just a fish!" After that, Don went to see Ty while I went back to work. When Don came back, he said that Ty explained that the Superintendent told him Hal Claymore didn't belong on the floor as a porter, because he was doing 20 to 40 as a sex offender! Wow! I wonder what Hal did to get that much time! And I'm also wondering how he managed to get the job working on the floor in the first place! I began feeling a bit better, but still uneasy about the whole thing. I had started seeing my scheduled men again, when Claymore came into my office, and he was *angry*. I told him to come back later, after I had finished working. But all of a sudden, at 3:30, a man on the bench outside my door asked if I was going to see him soon? So I realized I wasn't anywhere near done yet! I ended up the day minus two reports and all flustered, because Claymore stopped again and said he felt I was responsible, in spite of my denial. Then Officer Riley stopped in again, and stressed to Don, who was there then, that he fears reprisals, both on residents and on himself. So much is involved here. It seems that Ty used to be Superintendent and was demoted in a staff shakeup. On top of learning all that, (that I really didn't want to know!) I heard on the way out, that Mark is planning to quit his job as cadre. What a mess, especially with charges of racism touching everyone involved. Does all this make any sense? I'm having trouble sorting everything out!

Thursday, Dec. 18th

I felt a bit better today, though I had slept very little last night. Don stopped to see if I was OK, and said at noon that he could tell by my face that I was upset. I finished up my two holdover cases, and then let Lou take Dolman, who is now in Five West, the punishment block and one place in the prison I will probably never be allowed to go---nor would I really want to. It is commonly known as "the hole" and is taking the place of that cell block in the yard that was taken down. Lou says he has known Dolman since Boy's Training School, and that he just always wants all the privileges.

Anyway, I barely finished seeing my men by noon, because Steve called me to come upstairs. It seems I was supposed to make out a form to commit the man Edward and I saw together yesterday, to have him taken to segregation as dangerous. And then Steve pronounced that if the man had killed someone, I'd have been responsible! That got my back up, and I said I felt I should have been trained in such procedures, or that Ronald should have told me this when I discussed the man with him! But finally, though belatedly, I made out the form. However, at noon I found the man *sitting outside my office!* When I asked, I was told he'd been on Housekeeping duty on second or third gallery today!!! What idiot decided he could do that?? Long-standing grudges, racism, incompetence--- it's hard to know who to trust, even who to call on if there is trouble. Steve also said that he's tired of hearing about "humanity" in the prison--- he's concerned with the people on the street! Well, so am I! But is punishment, or treatment, more effective in changing people around??? It does come down to that, doesn't it?

There was a Christmas party, of sorts, at noon. Clinical Services were there, so there was some strain. I sat by Dr. Bartholomew, the CSU honcho, for a while, but felt uncomfortable. Then I moved to sit with our group. Fa la la.

The afternoon was hectic. I barely finished on time. There was good news, though. Jimmy came in to tell me that Claymore was not the only one who lost his job. It's a general tightening up, in part because of yesterday, and in part because of anticipation of trouble at Christmas. And Claymore came down, and in a very gentlemanly way, told me he didn't blame me now, at all. So--- all ended well--- for now!

Friday, Dec. 19th

I was in classification this morning with Steve--- we saw 55 men! I felt badly because we sent a number of men to inappropriate places in the system, due to lack of bed space. I am beginning to understand what all Steve is up against, with the overcrowding. He has to keep a racial balance in the institutions, too. All of this means extra work, and it was hard keeping track of everything today.

I forgot my keys today, so had to get help from Officer Bishop to get in my office!

Don has asked me and Jimmy to go with him to De Ho Co Monday, so I had to get all my things ready for the trip--- dictaphone, test materials, etc. I also saw three men this afternoon--- and finished early! So I went upstairs to see Dr. Chakraborty's "immediate feedback" machine for remedial reading. He won $5000 from the U.N. for it. He is quite a remarkable man. Just as I was going back to my office, Edward and Jimmy came along and said Ronald wanted the three of us to see a guy in the bubble who seems suicidal. Since it was almost quitting time, I carried my stuff up with me. We interviewed the boy up there. Or rather, Edward and Jimmy did. He wouldn't say much at first, just stared. But then he finally admitted he wanted to kill himself, and said he would, first chance he had. Jimmy was verbally quite rough with him and I didn't get a word in. Of course, we had to send him to the tender care of Top Six. But as they led him out, he looked at me, and I'll never forget that silent plea for help--- and I didn't, couldn't, say or do anything! And it's Christmas and he's only 18 and scared---

And the loudspeakers on top of the Seven Block building sadistically continue to blare out, "I'll Be Home for Christmas," over and over again.

Monday, Dec. 22nd

Today was spent at famed (or infamous) De Ho Co, the women's prison. We picked up our things at the bubble, and then Don drove us in a state car (Don and I in front, Jimmy and Mabel in back.) We had a guard screen between us, and the back doors were the kind that won't open from the inside. We had to show our IDs at the gate when we arrived. I was surprised to find the institution out in the country and it seemed to have a pleasant atmosphere. We were in the main building while there. I took over a large office with a window(!), and even a stereo (which I didn't use, of course). I was supposed to do reports on five women, but only managed three, as the interruptions were many--- phone, Don, training Barry (a new man?) in the afternoon. I saw two interesting women in the morning. One 34 year old was a chronic thief and drug addict, but a program there called Shar House seems to be helping her. The second woman had a horrible past--- rape, etc. and was pretty schizoid.

We ate upstairs, and there were tablecloths, and women to wait on us! The food was good, too. Don was into analyzing Jimmy at the dinner table, and I felt really sorry for him. He and I talked about it later.

The afternoon didn't go as well, and I only interviewed one person. Then I discovered the keys to the office I was using had disappeared. Actually, the lady whose office it was, had picked them up, but it delayed us for some time, straightening it out. We returned to SPSM in time to check out, though. Don apparently "interviewed" the women that Jimmy and I saw today, out in the hall before we left, and I figure he'll be combing our reports for flaws. So I plan to redo several. I'm paranoid!

Tuesday, Dec. 23rd

I was handed six folders this morning, plus I wanted to redo yesterday's reports. I finally had drafts finished of two of those, and then I finished with two and a half from today, before Jimmy and Edward stopped for me. We decided to go out, not up, today for lunch. While we were eating, they explained to me for a half hour, how paranoid I am for thinking Don would be testing *us* on our De Ho Co reports, and how my insecurity is to blame, etc. etc. We got back only to discover we'd forgotten all about staff meeting! Ronald was a bit upset. He called me later, and I went over to his office in the yard for my two month evaluation— which was a good one. We just talked about the logistics of my doing group therapy soon. Anyway, I got behind this afternoon and never quite caught up, especially since I became aware that the last man was trying to con me! I was onto him, and let him know it, and we ended up laughing. That was just as Edward called to tell me we had seven minutes to go to get out of the block. He and Jimmy are great! I had one very insolent, hostile resident today, who just walked into my office without being called. When he left, he slammed the door, and Jimmy came bounding in, ready to report him. The man was doing life for first degree murder, but although he was angry, I didn't really feel he was threatening me, so I let it go.

Anyway, as we got to the bubble, there sat Don, going through our De Ho Co reports! Ha! He said mine was OK, then turned to Jimmy and began tearing his apart! Poor Jimmy, Don really seems to have it in for him. Jimmy and Edward wouldn't mind De Ho Co duty--- and had pressured Don to check out about that possibility. Don said they're being considered, and are to go over there the first week in January. He also told me that he wants me to go back again when he does.

Oh yes, Hal Claymore stopped in and wants me to help him arrange it so he can get married!! (?) Also, one man I had seen, and who is to be sent to Ionia, started a grievance--- which got nowhere, but I had to talk with him at length. So I managed to get behind on work once again. Oh well, tomorrow I have off!!

And a Merry Christmas to all!

Friday, Dec. 26th

Today was really strange. Almost no one was around. It was snowing hard this morning and the roads were really bad. Ronald drove and we made it OK, but Dr. Chakraborty had an accident and was hurt. He came in for his group but was heading for the doctor this afternoon.

Anyway, I saw six men today, but didn't get the last report finished. At four, I went to the bubble office, and found it locked, and there was no one around except residents (trustys). It was a weird feeling! One resident told me today that he'd heard about me. I asked what he had heard and he said that I was "one of the best psychs." Flattery! But the men do seem more and more polite, in general.

Don wrote a letter stating my position and salary today, but seemed a bit annoyed with me. Perhaps he didn't like it that I asked him if Fred, my former co-worker at the Crisis Center, could visit me at Seven Block on Friday next week. Fred is a social worker and was in charge of the Crisis Center in St. Johns where I worked for awhile. I had felt it was an appropriate request, but maybe I was overstepping by asking.

Monday, Dec. 29th

I was busy all day today. Owen sat in with me most of the morning. First, though, Paul stopped to talk with me about his Christmas with his girlfriend, Rose. Poor Paul. I had a report from Friday to finish, and then saw two other men before lunch, plus a drop-in, a visit to see Hal on first gallery, and discussions with Owen, who is new. I had told Paul I'd eat with him outside, but when 11:30 came and went and I couldn't reach him, I went upstairs with Owen, and Don joined us.

Apparently, Edward and Jimmy had expected me outside, too, and stopped in to find out what had happened! Am I popular, or what? Probably "what"!

I was in Earl's office this afternoon when a great commotion arose in the cell block. As one man, Earl, Steve, Mark, Dan, and Don headed out the door. Yours truly was "chicken" and stayed rooted to the spot! When they came back, Don told me it was harmless. A seventeen year old overt homosexual, who looks like a girl, had just come on the floor---

I saw a lifer today. He was a brother of the insolent guy Jimmy was so upset about the other day. However, this brother had done the cold-blooded killing. I couldn't get through to him at all. So I started talking with him about programs, and asked him what he needed? I nearly went into shock when I heard him say, "A little love." I asked him to repeat it, and it was the same thing, followed by other obscenities. I stayed outwardly cool, laughed, and said I imagined so, but we'd better get to more practical matters. And that was it.

Tuesday, Dec. 30th

It was astonishing--- I got through with everything today! I'll admit that one man was not around to be seen, however. The files were thinner ones, and that helps. This morning, Jimmy blew in to ventilate. Don has been riding him pretty hard, and told him today that he'd have to improve his dictation. I guess the typing pool has complained. He blew up at Don--- who said he'd see him after he came back from De Ho Co.

Well, at noon I ate with Edward, Jimmy, Paul, etc. and took a lot of ribbing about missing lunch with them yesterday, but all friendly. Then we had staff meeting. Lou was more obstreperous than usual. Come to find out, he'd been robbed (burglarized) at home of some $10,000 and one of his guns had been used to kill someone. No wonder he was upset---- but why take it out on us?? Anyway, the ethical concerns committee presented proposals for better ways of doing parole evaluations. Good. There is quite an outcry over crimes committed by parolees. If only the public knew how the evaluations are done--- in cleaning closets, and so on.

I was just recalling--- during the commotion yesterday when I was alone in Earl's office, Mark came back in to stay with me. I asked him about his Christmas, and he reported he'd hung up his stocking, but just got a big, black cigar--- and just then everyone else came back in. I don't think I want to know, but it surely sounds symbolic, to me.

Jimmy and Edward seem to feel that I'm privileged, because I'm allowed to bring Fred into the block on Friday, and it makes me feel badly that they feel that way.

I was actually *finished* by 3:45 today.

Wednesday, Dec. 31st

This was a half day, great! I had my morning three done by 11:15 and then hung around with Jimmy and Edward until 11:45. But I forgot to take my files up to the bubble! Don stopped in to chat awhile. He seems a lonely man. The guys kidded me, when we were in Earl's office, about my looking like a snowflake in my white coat today, and I brought down the house when I said, "But I'm not cold,"--- All in good fun, but I should know when to shut up by now! Fortunately, only psych staff were present.

From the Director

During the past few years, the Michigan Department of Corrections has become more acutely aware of public dissatisfaction with the criminal justice system's ability to make substantial inroads against crime.

With regard to the correctional system in particular, the public feels now it has been deceived; that a commitment to prison should have meant an individual would never again commit a crime because he would be rehabilitated. Instead, much of the citizenry now believes that parolees and ex-prisoners are a major part of the problem.

This feeling of betrayal — that rehabilitation was supposed to work, but didn't — has resulted in several reactions. One says if rehabilitation doesn't work, then prisons are no good and should be abolished; the other says if prisons don't rehabilitate, then we shouldn't parole offenders who aren't rehabilitated.

The first reaction — to abolish prisons — which is less likely to gain substantial support, ignores the fact that some individuals must be isolated from society because they are dangerous and violent. It offers no protection for the public.

The second, which would lock up all prisoners longer, has gained more support, but it offers public protection only at an enormous human and economic cost.

In Michigan about one parolee in 100 will commit a very serious crime involving death or serious injury to the victim. Yet most legislative proposals require that we lock up all 100 persons longer to try to prevent the one violent crime.

We believe this alternative offers an essentially unjust, wasteful and ineffective solution to the problem.

Unless we are able to present a reasonable and balanced alternative for public protection, however, some of the harsh, public reaction to crime will be enacted into law because there seems to be no other solution.

The department has been re-examining its concepts and reason for being and has reconfirmed its single and overriding justification for being — protection of the public.

We have now concluded that the greatest failure of the corrections system is not its inability to rehabilitate or to deter, but its failure to realize its full potential in testing and screening out the possibly dangerous.

This ability has been here from the beginning, but we only saw it demonstrated clearly for the first time when we were evaluating our community corrections centers.

The 1974 evaluation was designed, in part, to find out whether these community

From D.O.C. brochure. Used by courtesy of the Michigan Department of Corrections.

Figure 13 - Perry Johnson had fair and balanced views that I liked.

residential centers were effectively screening persons who were dangerous to the community from those who were not.

What was discovered was that a total of 71 percent of the cases performed consistently at the centers and on parole. That is, they either failed both or succeeded at both. This, according to the authors of the evaluation, is evidence that an offender's performance at a center is an indicator of how well he will do on parole.

The bonus was that such screening occurred at little risk to the public because of the close supervision given residents which meant that failing residents could be returned to prison before they committed a more serious crime.

Parole contracts, too, promise to be an effective screening and testing method and their worth in that respect is about to be evaluated.

Screening has always been part of the parole process, but the Parole Board has often had to make its decisions based on haphazard, incomplete and subjective information.

Since parole decisions should be more on target if better information for such decisions is provided, the department is in the process of developing computer technology and research to try to find predictors of recidivism and particularly violent recidivism.

If such predictions can be made, instead of locking up 100 to prevent the one violent crime, we may be able to incarcerate only a few.

Although we are barely in our infancy of our ability to make such predictions, we are encouraged by other experiments out-of-state and the fact that the system already has some implicit screening abilities.

But even when screening techniques are made more effective, they will need to be supplemented with ongoing evaluations of each person's actual performance. A system which relies solely on actuarial techniques, typologies or other statistical mechanisms will perpetuate the sin of tacking lables on people from which they cannot extricate themselves.

The problem has been, however, that performance within the prison system is a notoriously bad indicator of performance after release. The individual who is "con-wise" can readily make it through without deviating in his intentions from a confirmed criminal career. We must, therefore, change the system to accurately test an individual's behavior.

As it stands now, the system neither allows nor demands responsible behavior. It was not set up to do that, but to treat a mass of people in the most economical way possible; this normally excludes any recognition of individual differences and needs.

A system which differentiates between individuals and allows for inmate participation in the determination of what kinds of programs will be most relevant is more likely to provide the sort of test that approximates the outside world.

Insofar as we can provide programs and activities that continually require responsibility, we also can monitor changes in behavior.

We should not require people to participate in educational programs or counseling if these have no relevance to their antisocial behavior. There may be some for whom no treatment programming is relevant, and it should not be required of them.

To require an individual whose only problem is assaultiveness and lack of contro to complete high school is frivolous. To allow him to do so is appropriate, however.

Beyond what we can do in an institution, we also will be looking at expanded use of programming in the community, not simply because the community is the best place to rehabilitate people, even though it might be, but because it is the best place to provide a true test of readiness to behave responsibly.

A considerable reorientation will be necessary to achieve the kind of system we are talking about. We must now make a systemwide commitment to move in that direction.

The challenge of trying to meet these new goals in the midst of a growing prison population will be at times overwhelming. The temptation will be to leave the system as it is until "times are better," but no time is more appropriate than now. We cannot wait, and we will not wait for changes to be forced on us; we must make our own changes based on our best abilities and knowledge.

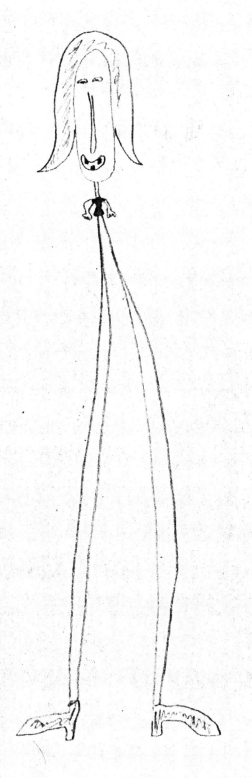

Figure 14 - One of the psychological tests instructed the resident to "draw a person". Some of the art work produced was interesting to interpret! Drawing shown is actual size.

1976

Today was the day Fred came. He was really nervous--- scared, actually, and was big enough to admit it. Don gave him a pass that took him all through the prison, even up to eat in the OD. I don't feel that the others appreciated his being there, but the inmates didn't seem to mind. Actually, all the residents today were quite pleasant. I fell behind this morning, and Edward saw one of my men. Fred and I did take time to talk, of course. Fred said after lunch that he likes Paul especially.

My dictaphone isn't fixed yet, and I wish they would hurry up, as the one Don gave me as a temporary substitute is really worse than the other. As we were leaving this afternoon, a man I saw Wednesday stopped me again to ask for help getting a job in R&GC (Seven Block). I'd been told that they wanted his report right away for parole evaluation. But when I woke up in the night last night, I suddenly remembered that I had done a rather unfavorable report on him recently, without much new evidence, as his psych reports in the files were all old ones. I worried about it through most of the weekend, after that.

Monday, Jan. 5th

Fred tells me he is sure something is going to happen to me. However, I guess I just don't have the certainty about it that I used to. So many men speak to me by name, now, as I go in or out of the block, and it's a good feeling. Of course, the population in Seven Block is constantly changing. After several weeks in quarantine, the men we have processed are sent out to other institutions or placement at SPSM, and we often pass by sheriff's deputies in the bubble as they unlock the chains on men newly arrived from around the state. Mark tells me that the reason the catcalls have subsided is that the men in R&GC have learned to respect me. Whether true or not, hearing it made me feel wonderful, of course. But I must never forget that this is a very dangerous place.

I only saw three men today, as I was scheduled to sit in with Bob's therapy group this afternoon from 2:00 on. After seeing the morning's men, I had a little time, so when Jimmy called from Earl's office and said, "Come on down," I did. Jimmy and Edward are my great friends now, and having friends is so important in here. They include me in everything, bless 'em, and I do enjoy their company. They are not at all alike, as Jimmy is much more casual and "street savvy", and Edward is a bit rigid and professorial, but in spite of our differences, we get along well. I just don't see Bob around as much since he moved to his new office. I gather that he often skips lunch altogether in order to complete all his work. That is too bad. I wish he would join all of us more often.

Bob's sex offender therapy group, held in a subhall room, was interesting. It was weird, hearing women referred to as a species apart--- I really felt sorry for some of the men, but not for one who's means of communicating with women is by strangling them until their eyes bulge! Bob and Ronald said there were differences in the group due to my being there, as they were more open and courteous to each other. I really got up tight at one point, when it looked as though they were going to question me. But otherwise, I enjoyed it. I wonder how I will do as a group leader?? I went with Bob and Ronald for coffee afterwards, and forgot to pick up my purse, containing my car keys, from the bubble before the shift change tonight. Wally (an officer from the next shift) was nice enough to reopen for me.

Oh, Paul stopped in today to ask me if I'd like to get into square dancing, which he heard me say I used to love. I really can't, but it was nice of him. Don stopped in too, mostly to talk about my hang-ups! I'll have to admit, he's pretty perceptive, and he's the boss, but I do wish he would stop his analysis of me!

Oh yes, the man I worried about all weekend did go for his parole evaluation today. I heard them page him from the desk. I felt a little better about my report after I talked with Lou, whose philosophy is that you should never think about a report again, after having done your best at the time. But I guess I'm not really made that way.

Today started off calmly enough. I decided to catch up, by reading all my old reports, and so on. But as a result, I got a late start with today's work. And then I had a case I couldn't quite figure out, when trying to do the report, so asked Jimmy for help. It turned out I had been conned--- and by a schizophrenic yet! I felt like a real amateur, but he certainly had been convincing. Anyway, I had to put my third man on recall in order to go to lunch early, as it was staff meeting day. I ate with the guys, which is always a fun break and helps keep me on track with working here. The staff meeting seemed more congenial than usual. I'm to be on OPS (Out Patient Services) in the subhall every Thursday. This will be different, and I hope the guards will let me in when I'm by myself!

In the afternoon, I was to have had court again, but Ferris came in and said he'd take it, which was great as I hate court duty. I saw two men by 3:00, then I went to the office to ask Dan to send my last man in, but he said to forget it--- and so I did. I spent the hour cleaning house. I put up a poster, read my mail (kites), talked with Dr. C. and even left a few minutes early. But after a comparatively good day, I was all "shook up" when I read the critical incident reports in the Spectator (inmate newspaper). Dolman, the man I let Lou see last week but who wanted to see me, jumped off 4th gallery of Five West and is in bad shape. I didn't help him--- and Lou had said he was only looking for an easy place to do his time! I feel bad.

I was in classification this morning, although Jimmy wanted it. I figured I needed a break as much as he did! It is always interesting, and wasn't as hectic today. In fact, we finished a bit before 11:00, so Steve and I sat and talked about testing. He's not a psychologist, of course, so I tried to explain how much the psych testing results help us in understanding the men we see. Then both of us went to lunch with the group. We attempted to all eat together in the OD by pushing two of the tables together, and the resident in charge there had a "conniption fit"! "Not allowed!" So when two of our group left, we put them back as they were before. But just then, Todd and Owen came and we pushed them back together again, and *wow*, the resident really got angry! So Edward and I left about then, and I guess it all tapered off after that.

Dan Hillier, a new staff member, sat in with me this afternoon. He is interesting, and also was very helpful. We saw two members of a motorcycle gang that had raped a 16 year old. The first was a follower, but one (age 36) was a sadistic, woman-hating latent schizophrenic. But both seemed quite "together" during their interviews today. And they both denied any guilt.

But I ended up the day on a more cheery note, when I interviewed a black kid who's tried very hard, and who, I think, may make it. I do hope so. Oh, and Hal stopped. He said he hoped I wouldn't be mad if he told me something--- he thinks he loves me! I told him it's because I'm the only woman around (!) and that he will find someone nice after he gets out--- (I wonder when *that* will be?) He's been in disciplinary, (Five West) and told me of the bare cells, no clothes--- I must get a look at his file sometime. Or maybe I really don't want to know!

Thursday, Jan. 8th

Even though today was different, it wasn't restful. Ronald scheduled me and Dr. C. to go to Cassidy Lake and Camp Waterloo. Both are minimum custody, of course. We drove with Ronald and Frank Griffith, and didn't go into Seven Block at all. We waited in the lobby for everyone to gather, then took off in a state car. We were there by 9:15, and went through some beautiful country on the way. The Cassidy Lake setting is gorgeous, with rolling land, pines, cabins set back from the lake. It was a glistening, cold day. I sat in on the morning group, and it was a very slow mover. I felt Frank wasn't helping much, (it's his group) though I guess I would probably do worse! One black kid was very "flip" and talked constantly. But toward the end of the session, I caught a look into his eyes at an unguarded moment, and I was really shocked at the hurt I saw there. He hung around for quite a while afterward, but didn't say anything. I almost went over to him but didn't, and I wish I had.

We went to lunch in Chelsea. It was a Dairy Queen, and I had the worst hamburger I have ever had! But it was nice being with the guys. I guess it doesn't seem strange to me, being friends with a number of men, and the only female there. After all, I was the first girl allowed to take a class in Mechanical Drawing when I was in High School (I had to go to the principal and fight for that privilege!) There I learned to cope with a lot of good-natured teasing from both my classmates and the teacher. And later, just after High School, my job at Cornell's Photo Science Lab meant I was the only girl working with the all-male photographers. I did resent being required to fix the coffee for coffee break each day, as it was considered "woman's work!" However, I felt they were all my friends and learned that being teased only meant that they accepted me. So in Seven Block, once again I am in a similar situation with an all-male staff (so far!)

After lunch, we drove back to Cassidy Lake, and Dr. C. and I were given the grand tour by one of the staff there. They have very impressive facilities. At the school, two young men I'd recommended for camp when they were in quarantine came up to me, delighted to see me and they were sure I remembered them. That felt good! (There are rewards once in a while!) We spent quite a bit of time in the reading room and library because of Dr. C's interest. The staff seemed nice--- all except the treatment director, who was very disparaging because of our "poor referrals!" We finished the tour just as the other group session was ending, and heard a young burglar bragging about how much money he gets, and how he has thousands stashed away--- and how he carries a pistol to protect himself. I wouldn't bet on how long it will be after his release before he will be with us in Seven Block again!

Then it was time to drive to Camp Waterloo, which was another nice place. We had to do parole evaluations. I was lucky, and interviewed a man sentenced for second degree murder seven years ago, and who hasn't done anything wrong since, at least on the record. He seemed like a very nice man now, and I felt good about telling him I was recommending parole. He was so pleased.

Friday, Jan. 9th

I was only given four men to see today, so I sort of took my time--- delightful! Staff meeting was scheduled for 2:45. I went up to eat at 11:00 with the guys and Don was already there. He asked us if anything was happening on Seven Block, and we said "No, should there be?" And he told us there was to be an alert. An alert means a "lockdown" where all the residents are locked in their cells, and no one can go into or out of the prison. At noon, the sirens began and it was eerie--- and deafening! I figured we wouldn't be able to go back into the block, but such was not the case. We were able to go back through Six Block, and when we reached Seven, Ronald called to us from Control. We all went up there, and he told us that when there is an alert, we are considered custodial staff, and are to assist the officers any way we can. So--- one of us went off with each set of two officers, but I was assigned to go with Officer Danny Elliottson, who has been very nice to me. We searched Dan and Mark's offices, the kitchen, and the testing rooms. I *hated* going through those desks in the offices, it seemed like such an invasion of privacy of people you had come to know. I had a splitting headache by then, so when that part was finished, I sat on the bench for a while. Then two officers asked if I'd like to come along to help them search fourth gallery, or if I'd rather supervise? I said if it was a choice, I'd supervise! (Fourth gallery is scary at *any* time! Just viewing base five stories below, from that height, is enough to unsettle me!) So I spent a while talking with Will (a new cadre) at the desk. I couldn't help but notice the hoots and catcalls as I had walked with Danny. Will said one of the men told him the other day that Mrs. Becker really is "a nice lady." It was nice of Will to tell me that, but I wonder what the men will think after today? This sort of thing does not jibe with our roles as helpers, and I really dislike being called on to do it. However, it was good getting acquainted with Will. He seems very nice. He said he had almost finished college on the outside.

After that, Edward and Owen came in and we talked until the lockup (or lockdown) was over. This was the first one in a year and a half, they say. The officers collected lots of loot from the cells and elsewhere--- weapons, drugs, clothing, dishes, and so on.

I had recommended Muskegon for a man this morning, and later, after talking with Steve (who still criticizes my placements), I realized that the man had lied to me and had taken me in. I went back and changed my recommendation to "The Hill" (Ionia Max)--- that was a close one! As I said, I know I'm not infallible!

I went to staff meeting at 3:00. Don didn't show up until 3:30, presumably because he brought guests from Voc. Rehab. They didn't get a very friendly welcome, from Don at least. The Dolman thing was brought up by Ethan. Lou let him know he'd called Top Six about Dolman, and had been told then that they didn't want Dolman up there! What a shame there are so many bad feelings between the two units. It is hurtful to everyone.

Monday, Jan. 12th

This was an interesting day, with ups and downs. I received a blast from Ronald right away in the car, when I mentioned I thought we should protest about our dual role at the general shakedown last Friday. Undaunted, I went to Jimmy, Edward, Dr. C., and Dan, for opinions, and all said they'd sign a protest letter to Don if I'd draft it. So I decided I'd stick my neck out and do just that. However, by noon, when I ate lunch with the guys, I found all my support had vanished--- it was too much of a risk for Edward and Jimmy. I told them I was angry. It was touchy and I really did feel hurt. Tonight Ronald said he'd heard I was upset, and apologized for snapping at me. Actually, he had heard that I might be upset from Don, who surmised this because I failed to say "Hi" to him this morning! Anyway, Ronald and I talked it out and he agreed we shouldn't have to act as cops, and he will bring it up himself at staff.

This morning, I sat in on Paul's group in the academic school. It is rather scary up there, and even getting up the stairs off the subhall crosswalk in order to get there, made me apprehensive. There were actually very hostile stares. The group was interesting, though. They talked of sex the whole time, and wanted to learn how women feel about men who have participated in homosexual activities. It was both funny and touching. Paul and I had coffee after. Poor Paul, he spent the whole 45 minutes on the way to work today telling me about his problems with his girlfriend.

This afternoon I had three men and got a late start due to relieving Earl at noon. (I hadn't realized it was my turn again!) Steve spent the hour with me, and Jimmy and Edward stopped in also (feeling sheepish about yesterday, I believe.) One man I saw this afternoon was a child abuser who beat his two year old to death (he was a denier) and then there were two Mexicans who were picked up on Stoll Road near where I live, selling marijuana. I visited with one man quite a while. He said I was "a beautiful lady." It's nice to hear--- but hard to take seriously. I'm really not that gullible.

Edward reports they shot a gun into the cell block during a fight this afternoon (while I was out talking with the office about a discrepancy in my pay check.) He said that it scared him out of his wits, it was so loud! I know there is an officer back there with a gun trained on the block constantly, but you do tend to forget, as you go about daily duties. They say the first shot is a blank, but if that isn't enough, the second shot is real.

Tuesday, Jan. 13th

Today was a "regular" day, if any are! I saw my assigned men in the morning. I knew that the staff meeting was going to conflict with my sitting in for Earl at lunchtime, so I went down to check with him about it. Before I could say anything, he said, "No, you don't have to relieve me this noon." I said, "That's pretty good mind-reading, you'd make a good psychologist!" He replied, "Well, I've thought of it, but decided I don't really mind working for a living."

I was asked by Ronald to be recorder for staff meeting. It went better than usual (Lou used restraint!). Ronald brought up the protests over the shakedown, and it was discussed pretty thoroughly. The upshot was *Jimmy* and *Edward* volunteered to draft a protest! Ha!

I went with Prentis after staff to have an extra key made for my office, so he can use it sometimes, after I have left at night. The locksmith's quarters are below SPSM in the basement, and it is very dark and scary down there. The locksmith seemed surprised to see me there. Me too!!

I had hoped to see Don this afternoon about (maybe) being gone Thursday, and he said he'd be at his office, but I never did catch him in. When we got out tonight, it had snowed about 6 inches and was still coming down. Paul was a real sweetie and drove for me (maybe it was self-defense!) The roads were a mess. The last 10 miles alone, to get home from Lansing, were awful, but I made it.

I had to put a man on recall this morning. I always hate to do that, but I just didn't go fast enough, and had to have him relocked and rescheduled to see another time. I did spend quite a while talking with a 17 year old who needed someone to listen. Also, Jimmy called me to come up to classification, too, because I'd sent the one Mexican guy inside because of assaults, but they had been dismissed. I goofed--- but I'm glad it was in that direction.

I had to get someone at lunch to volunteer to walk me back early because of relieving Earl again. Steve was nice enough to do so. I had time then, to talk with Mark while in the office. He is an interesting young man. He still has two years to serve, but he says his attitude has changed a lot, in part thanks to Don's help. While I was there, Earl's new desk arrived and I helped get that settled in place. I had put in a bid to get his old one, but (a) it wouldn't fit through my office door, and (b) it was the same size as mine anyway. Oh well. Hal called down from first gallery to assure me *he* could get it through the door for me!

Store day is always bedlam. I have to go beyond Earl's office toward the ramp by myself to call my men, and the noise and disorder throughout the block is bad. Dan Hillier stopped in for coffee. And Paul held us up about 20 minutes tonight to finish his reports.

Friday, Jan. 16th

Almost every day is different in some way. This morning, I had group with Frank from 10:00 to 12:30, and was scheduled for court from 12:30 on. Beyond that, I was supposed to relieve Earl at lunch, which was an impossibility. I started off seeing one man, but before I could get into it, Steve arrived, questioning one of my reports. He suggested I should consult someone. I tried Ronald, who was not in, and then called Bob. He said "soon"--- but then I had trouble locating the man's psych file. I finally got everything together and talked with Bob--- but he also "passed the buck" and said to see Ronald. I really did feel that I was right--- the man was either a really bad actor or psychotic, and probably both. Anyway,

PSYCHOLOGICAL SERVICES STAFF MEETING

January 13, 1976

Staff Members Present: Drs.   , Walsh,   ,
Messrs.   ,   ,   ,   and Ms. Becker.

It was decided that the duty of recorder for weekly staff meetings will rotate
among staff members and the order will be determined alphabetically. Jean Becker
will act in this capacity during the month of January, and will be followed by
Mr.   in February.

Dr.   explained that the order of priority as to participation in various
programs should be determined according to the judgment of the staff members,
but with priority given to Parole Contracts.

In response to requests from staff members to learn more about treatment programs
at the various institutions, Dr.   reported that we will soon be having
reports concerning programs underway at SPSM.   · will attempt to
obtain information for us on the programs at Ionia.

There was positive reaction by most staff to the suggestion that there be a
rotating assignment of duty therapist for the unit. This way all staff members
would share the responsibility of attending to emergencies, and the uncertainty
as to who should be called would be alleviated.

An explanation was given concerning the duties of staff assigned as court Advocate.
When an Advocate is requested, the Desk notifies   , who then assigns that
duty to staff on a rotating basis through written notice in the mailboxes. The
individual so appointed will normally have been scheduled to sit in court, and
will use the time following this session to prepare for his role as Advocate the
following session. If additional time is needed,   should be notified
so that scheduling can be shifted accordingly.

There was a good deal of discussion concerning the use of Psychological Services
Staff as custodial personnel during institutional procedures such as the general
shakedown of January 9. The concern was expressed that our role as treatment staff
is hindered by such activities, and that the taking away of non-harmful convenience
items especially tends to allienate residents. Many staff members stated that they
would not hesitate to aid custodial staff in any real emergency situation, although
there was some disagreement on this because of staff's lack of training and medical
coverage, and possible liability in case of injury. There was apparent unanimity
in the opinion that our concerns should be presented to the Administration, and
discussion then centered around whether this should be a matter for the Ethical
Concerns Committee to handle.   suggested that a new committee be
set up to present our views, in writing, and find out existing policies.
          and   volunteered to act as members of this
committee.

        stated that the proposed procedures for parole evaluations and reduced
custody screening have not been submitted, but suggested that input must be received
by the morning of January 14 in order to be included for consideration. We were
also informed that the time differential between the minimally acceptable and
ideal procedures as drafted by the Ethical Concerns Committee are very slight.

                         Jean Becker - Recorder

JB/dmc

Warden-Employee Meeting with Group Two
Wednesday, April 14, 1976

1. What can be done about the pigeons that abound around the institution? They have a definite adverse affect on sanitation and health problems.

   Answer: We recently received a supply of strychnine pigeon bait which has been placed on the roofs of the various institutional buildings. This is a never-ending problem, but we hope to reduce the population considerably with this new bait.

2. The Department's policy of hiring women is creating a serious problem throughout the institution. Every move the women make requires an escorting male employee, thus depriving his assignment of needed manpower when we are already short of manpower. Should trouble arise, the male employees will have to look after the women besides trying to do what might be necessary to restore order and save their own skin at the same time. Can you do anything to impress this fact on the Department?

   Answer: Permit me to quote from Policy Directive PD-DWA-03.01, "Affirmative Action Personnel Policy":

   "Historically, women have been excluded from employment in correctional facilities as probation and parole officers dealing with male clients, in many cases, without justification. As a matter of fairness and equity, women must not be excluded from jobs they are qualified for and capable of performing. Furthermore, the presence of women, where feasible, in correctional facilities for males is a healthy influence and contributes to more normal social conditions. This is not to obscure the fact that female employees face greater risk and dangers in some correctional facilities and that certain tasks cannot be performed by females if proper standards of decorum and personal privacy for clients are to be maintained..."

   I can appreciate the concerns of the male staff but the positions women are now holding at the Infirmary are absolutely necessary in upgrading the medical delivery system at the Institution.

3. What can be done about telephone procedure throughout the institution-- Department heads and Staff are answering the phones with a "yes" instead of identifying themselves and the assignment? Also, inmates are still using state phones to call whomever they so desire. The institutional phone directory is in sad shape as to correct numbers and complaints are becoming numerous. Can these be remedied in the near future?

Figure 15 - Previous page — A PSU staff meeting was always interesting. In this one we heard about our duties as Advocates in court sessions held in Seven Block, and our concern about being used as "Custody" during "shakedowns".

Figure 16 - Above — Custody objects to the hiring of women, and Warden responds.

107

after court, I saw Ronald, and he backed me up on my report. But I don't suppose Steve will be convinced! I wonder why he continues to be so critical of me?

The morning therapy group with Frank was tense. One "easy-rider" type had it in for Frank because he hadn't got the man's parole evaluation in on time. He was *really* hostile and bitter. Frank handled it well--- "Don't try and make me perfect!"

Court, I continue to hate! They can't do much but give suspended sentences, anyway, because of lack of room. Danny (Officer Elliottson) explained the routine to me. Luckily Luke Stuart was on, and Wallace--- both are friendly officers. I managed to stand up to defend a few men, but mostly rubber-stamped the decisions--- and felt angry that I did!

Poor Hal stopped in again today and wants help. Lou says that Hal will *never* be able to get all the help *he* needs.

Don was very upset today. He was scheduled to have signed for a new house yesterday, but discovered just in time that burst pipes had ruined the whole place! He exploded about it at lunch.

I couldn't get into the bubble for a long while this noon, as it was full with ten or twelve new men having chains and cuffs taken off. They slide them under the door--- clunk, clunk.

Monday, Jan. 19th

This was the first day of the new training. It wasn't fun, but not too bad either. We split into groups of five. I didn't get time for much else except for reading my mail from the mailbox. More about all of this later.

Tuesday, Jan. 20th

I just couldn't cope with things today, emotionally. I started out with a "load of stuff" from home, and right away, things went wrong in group, too. Frank and Jimmy had an argument yesterday, and Frank appealed to Don, who proceeded to take Jimmy apart again, psychologically, in front of everyone. He was very threatening--- how Jimmy had to get his head together before he could help others. After, I had just time in the hall to tell Don I couldn't cope---when it was surely time for me to do just that! In the afternoon session, Don jumped right in again, with me designated as his partner, exploring his problems with staff. I felt like a robot, but kept spitting out answers according to the "You feel because" model, when suddenly Jimmy shouted out that Don was "crucifying Jean," and to "Stop it!" So Frank jumped in and took my place with Don, but he didn't really understand the situation. Fortunately, then they went out for that needed smoke break, and I told Don how I felt, which was hostile because of the way he treats Jimmy. He said he realizes now that his presence in the group (being our boss and all) threatened both me and Jimmy, so he would leave the group. So after the others came back, he presented this to everyone. They all agreed that Don should stay, and I told him my anxiety would go *up* sky high, if he left now! And so the day went on. Don avoided me from then on, and didn't even eat lunch with us. When we assembled in the afternoon, he had joined a different group. I "flunked" the training in the afternoon. I was to repeat the plagued "sentence map." I hate it! When we went back to the larger group, tempers were still hot, and Frank flared up at Jimmy again, out of all proportion.

It is strange how the residents pick up on things. Jimmy and Deemer (who was a resident formerly and has now been hired to do exit testing) both told me I was upset, even before anything had happened!

Obviously, I didn't have time to attend staff today, so I asked Dan Hillier to take the minutes for me.

Don says he has a splitting headache and I'm sorry about all of it, but I don't see what else I could, or should, have done. Or could I??

Wednesday, Jan. 21st

Every day is different--- or have I said that before? First thing this morning, I managed to find time to have Hal Claymore brought down so I could talk with him. I told him I'd read his file, but naturally, I didn't discuss the details of how he and his cronies tortured an old man to death for kicks. Anyway, he's always happy to talk, and seems unrealistically encouraged about his chances of spending the rest of his 20 to 40 years in reduced custody. He warned me about going into the galleries unescorted. I'm having difficulty putting this boy together with the horrendous thing he was involved in.

Our group met again, and went into a wrap up of the sessions. It amazed me--- all the positive comments. Jimmy leaned over and asked me in a whisper if I thought we should bring up any of the negative feelings. When we did, that brought Don into it, and Don involved me--- and he misquoted me, so I spoke up again, on Jimmy's behalf. Shortly after that, we took a break, and Jimmy leaned over and put his arm around me and said that that was the nicest thing anyone had ever done for him on the job. And just then, Lou blew up--- called us all hypocrites and lambasted each of us individually for being "too chicken-livered to tell the whole truth," and then he stormed out. After that, the rest of the session was uninspired but also uneventful. Thank goodness.

Afterward, outside, I talked with Bob, who said I voiced the concerns of a lot of the staff who don't ever speak up. As I think about what has taken place, I recall in the past being in therapy groups, leading therapy groups, and I was once in a weeklong "sensitivity" group where I was knocked down by the leader in front of the group, but so far, this week in "assertiveness training" has been the most divisive and potentially harmful group experience I have ever encountered!

Now Don is avoiding me like the plague. Except for Don, we ate upstairs and it was a good meal for a change! We asked how come, and our friendly cook up there retorted that he couldn't imagine--- and that it couldn't have anything to do with the state inspectors having just left----

Edward and Jimmy walked me up to Room 18 for Ethan's group in the Academic School. Ethan was late, so I sat and talked with his men for a while. They really dislike Ethan. The group was interesting. Ethan is hostile--- but good (is this possible?) After group, or nearly so, one man asked me for my feelings on what had gone on. And of all things, just then his pants split!! There was a hearty laugh by all! Oh, the men were concerned about Ethan's language in front of me. Ethan said he guessed that should be *my* concern, if I didn't like it. I went to Top Six with him after, and had a decent cup of coffee. I wonder why his office is in Top Six now? We talked for about a half hour, mostly nonspecific about his group, and then I brought up Don and the training. I wish I hadn't. Ethan hates Don's guts--- says he wouldn't give him water if he was dying of thirst—which says more about Ethan than it does about Don! Then he escorted me down the elevator. He said he felt I could do it alone, but said "George" (the elevator man) is a paranoid schiz, and at times while waiting for the elevator, you hear long conversations going on! Oh, while I was in Ethan's office, one young therapist came in and introduced himself. Then Monroe came in, and pulled my head over against him. Instant nausea. I should bite!

I got back to Seven Block and found sheets on my prospective group members. So once more, the controversy arose over whether I need an escort to go to and from group. Dan, a resident cadre, insisted that I do, and was stony cold about it. That made me really uneasy. In fact, a number of things did today. What's going on?

The guys left at 4:00, and I did too. I recalled one man, who was upset about it. We went to the cafeteria and batted things around, and I got silly and giddy. It must be a reaction to all the tension, for sure.

Thursday, Jan. 22nd

It certainly was quiet around Seven Block today, with Jimmy and Edward at De Ho Co with Don, and Ronald and Frank at Cassidy Lake. I took the opportunity to confront Dan about my need for an escort, and he came back loud and clear, that I DO need one. Well, I'm picking up a lot of vibrations to that effect. I hope there's not any *real* threat.

I was on classification this morning until 10:00. Then I interviewed one man, the one I'd recalled yesterday. I wish I hadn't. He was another conniver who talks your ear off. Steve was in a good mood, and told me my reports are among the most helpful of any of the staff. I told him he ought to say that into a tape recorder and save it for me!

I invited Dan Hillier to have lunch with me, and as luck would have it, fried chicken was on the menu, so we had to wait in line for at least 15 minutes--- right behind the chaplain! But it was worth it! I sat next to Deemer, who asked me if I would talk with him about some very intimate matters, at 3:00. I realize he's very sensitive about his past record and time as a resident, and he told me he trusts very few people. So I agreed. And then he never showed up! I did meet his wife and baby in the lobby, though. She's young, and very attractive.

This afternoon Steve decided I should be on security classification with him, so I recalled my men. It was interesting--- from a young cut-up, to a "queen." "She" couldn't imagine why "she'd" need protection. In a falsetto voice, makeup, and all. You do tend to forget it's really a man!

Well, at three, after Deemer didn't show up, I spent about 20 minutes talking with Jimmy, one of our clerks. He wants me to do therapy with him, piecemeal. He told me about Viet Nam, his girl, and so on.

I saw Ethan again. I really wish I hadn't talked with him about the group, the other day. I decided today that I'd "cool it" and not get so involved in staff issues for a while, after I talk with Don and try to settle the strained feelings.

Friday, Jan. 23rd

This morning was largely uneventful. I managed to see all three of my men and it was good to get back into the routine. I received a "Good morning" from Mark in my mailbox. I've been complaining when I never get mail! I also got my official three month rating. It was satisfactory in all ways--- and was signed by Don, too. My friend's grandson stopped in, as did Hal. Both were encouraged about one thing or another. I stopped to see Dan Hillier. He's OK today but has to be careful because of his open heart surgery.

I couldn't find anyone around at lunchtime. Mark offered to escort me, but I wasn't sure about *that* arrangement, so went out in front and had a chiliburger all by myself. So I was back at work by 12:00.

This afternoon, I went in Grier's office and found that Don was there with Earl. Earl joked about inviting me to a Mazola party(!) (I am using my imagination about what *that* is!) and just then Mark came in, and Mark's face turned really red. Was he embarrassed for me? As the only woman around here, I guess I've come to accept that this kind of teasing isn't meant negatively, if it's from staff that I have come to feel comfortable with. I hope I am right, and shouldn't be flaring up in righteous indignation!

I told Don I'd like to see him, so he came down to my office with me. I explained that I liked him, but was not apologizing for being honest. And then

I went on to clarify my feelings, a bit. He seems to feel he can't be my friend and my boss, too. I protested a little--- but it may be that he's right.

Cowboy came in later, ostensibly to fasten up my poster better (and pulled out a razor blade to cut the tape!) While there, he got around to what was on his mind--- He told me about all the hazards of being attacked by not being cautious enough--- like Sara. All I had heard about Sara before was that "she didn't work out," and I still haven't heard any details. But Cowboy assured me that nothing is going to happen to me while *he* is around.

Oh--- also, Don is a bit wary, and will not permit me to hold group in the Academic School. He told of a plot to rape one of the secretaries that had been foiled by an informer. This happened right out in the main part of the subhall crosswalk, near the stairs. And he told me that the stairwell to the school could be sealed off, just by closing the door, and I could be forced downstairs to the basement before anyone was aware of it. So he gave me a choice for my groups: Go with Betty to Cassidy Lake, have a group in Trusty, or conduct my group in the radio room in the subhall. I chose the radio room. I cannot go around scared--- but I don't intend to take unnecessary chances, either.

I had a resident kiss my hand as he left, this afternoon (I always do shake hands if there hasn't been too much hostility). I had been kidding a bit with him, and I guess he liked it. I also talked with a guy who shot and killed his wife. He is 41 and had no prior record. He seems to have a lot of good insights and was very likeable. And I saw one first offender with 20 to 30 for armed robbery. He was really hostile, and I couldn't reach him at all.

Monday, Jan. 26th

Today was more ordinary. In fact, I actually saw six men! It's hard to believe, since Brad Parker from De Ho Co sat in for a while, too. Nothing happened that was really astounding, all day long. Edward and Jimmy made my day a lot cheerier. Edward stopped in just to say "Hello" this morning. Don was in the lunchroom after work, planning more training (!) with Frank and Steve, again. They asked me if I had minded being the only woman--- then Steve said, "Of course, she's different." Don was colder than usual.

Today was--- well, aren't they all? I was able to see two men in the morning. One of mine had to be given to Lou because he was in the infirmary, which is far out in the yard. I had Brad in with me today because Don requested it. Apparently Don went home, sick. I took Brad up with me to eat in the OD, thereby affronting Edward and Jimmy, who declare I shall be ostracized for ten days, as a result. The food was *terrible*, once again. Oh, they say five residents have brought a suit over the cockroaches.

Ronald tells me Cowboy is OK, and if he says he'll watch over me, he will! He says I'd never believe it if I could see Cowboy in the exercise yard, getting guys to do *pushups!* (The fact that he is 6' 5" has something to do with it, perhaps?)

I received a letter (kite) from a man in Frank's group, asking to be in mine. Frank and Ronald say he's in love with me. I guess there is something to be said for being the only female around!

This afternoon, I went with Ronald (after staff meeting) to his group. They surely didn't love me! I was treated like a non-person. They discussed "women" but talked all around me. One man said, "All women are alike," and another said, "Yeah, all the ones I've known, are." So I spoke up and said, "Oh, not very experienced, eh?" I do know, though, that these are lonely guys adjusting to their outcast roles. Ronald and I went up for coffee after group. Then I went back to the block and dictated staff meeting minutes. I was really into it, for Paul had told staff that even Ronald earns less than prison school teachers!!

Jimmy (cadre) asked if I could call the four hospitals in Lansing to inquire as to whether his girl is there, having her baby. He can't locate her.

Wednesday, Jan. 28th

Today started out with Ronald running out of gas on the expressway! After muttering a few profanities, he started off down the highway with an empty gas can--- with the wind chill at -25 degrees! We didn't know if we'd ever see him again! First off, Paul decided we ought to hitchhike on in--- and a car stopped about as soon as we stuck out our thumbs. But then Paul changed his mind, because Ronald had left the car keys with us. So Paul and I found a blanket and tried to keep warm. One man stopped just to make sure we were all right. And eventually, Ronald came back. We were 45 minutes late. Paul and I kidded about our "blanket party!" I tried to recall one man due to lack of time, but was told that Don is pushing, so Lou took my man once again. Harry, the new man, was to have been with me all morning but was only there for a while. However, we got to talking, and I had to give Lou my third man also.

I ate lunch in the Rose Room (OD) again. Jimmy isn't feeling well. It was an ordinary afternoon--- as they go. Cowboy offered me a hard-boiled egg. I tried to see Don about taking time off tomorrow, but never did manage it because he wasn't in his office. I finally got him on the phone, just as he was heading home, feeling sick. There's a lot of that going around!

Thursday, Jan. 29th

I drove in alone today, so I could leave early. It was very slippery. I felt like I was coming down with a cold. Lou helped me out again today and now I am feeling guilty about letting him take my men so often. Anyway, I saw a black kid this morning--- he was just 18, and he sat there and sobbed because his people have rejected him. He had no word from them, even at Christmas time. He started off by asking if he could be placed near Detroit so he could have visitors--- then said, "No, it don't matter, nobody's going to come, anyway" and he began to cry. I was shook up about it, as I know there is so little I can do. However, I ended up running to first gallery anyway, to talk with Steve about the boy's placement--- but which has to be MTU (Ionia), Steve says, because he tried suicide in the County jail. It's hard to cope with all the misery, sometimes.

The next man was a manipulator, from beginning to end. He tried crocodile tears--- but a pending charge IS a pending charge! Anyway, both slowed me up. I ate with the guys upstairs as usual. Then we went back early, so I could get in one more man---- whose report I didn't quite finish before I had to leave at 1:30.

Monday was awful. I was just getting over a terrible cold, and it was 18 degrees below zero and bitter cold, when I left home at 6:45. In fact, my hands felt frostbitten, just getting underway. Unfortunately, *my* car's battery was dead--- it just gave a groan. So I had to take my husband's car. I noticed that the lights seemed a little dim, but didn't think much about it. I was the most nervous because the roads were very slippery, and I was hoping Paul would drive. But of all times, he never showed up! And Ronald stayed home sick. So I started out from Lansing alone. Then, horrors, I realized I had almost NO lights at all. Since I was out on the expressway by then, and streaks of light signified dawn, I kept going. But I had no *heat*, either! I made it all the way, but was late, and upset. At noon, I felt I *had* to know, so went out and started the car, and all seemed OK. At night after I punched out, the snow was coming down, and I had my fingers crossed. Oh, it started all right, and I backed out and was just about to the gate, when it stalled. It was no use--- the third time I tried, the battery gave up completely. So I turned on my blinkers and trudged back inside to have the desk call maintenance. Three calls and 50 minutes later, the truck showed up. The hot shot did no good, so I suggested it *might* be the butterfly valve, and voila! It was! So I took off and never stopped until I got home, in spite of a gas gauge on empty. (Then I spent the evening getting a battery for the car!)

Steve Ribby was nice. He gave me his phone number in case I ever need him. It looks like he'll be leaving, as he's had an interview and will be moving up the ladder. He asked me to sit down with him one noon this week. I thought I'd done something wrong--- again--- but he said he wanted to know how I had caught on so fast and others have so much trouble! I told him about the cards I made and put on rings, so I can have all the most useful information I may need, at my fingertips. He was very interested. He asked if I'd explain it to a training group Wednesday, and show them how it's done.

Don is feeling better. And he has bought a house.

Hal is still here, and stopped in one morning. He was going on and on and on and I could barely understand him--- and I was only half listening, but nodding (never safe in here!) when I realized he was suggesting we get together to celebrate after he gets out. Perish the thought!! But I consoled myself immediately with the thought of his 20 to 40 year sentence. However, two days later, he slipped in to tell me the appeal of his sentence had gone through!!

I also interviewed the first potential men for my therapy group, *alone* in the radio room on the subhall! I sort of flitted through when the crosswalk gate was open, before anyone stopped me. I'll admit I was a bit nervous, but everything ended up OK. I saw two of the men who'd been scheduled, another man said he didn't need anything, and a fourth (a hired killer and schizophrenic) didn't show up. I wasn't sorry! Well, that's a start, but I need quite a few more men before I can form a group.

Harry Churchill asked if I would help him, so I recalled a man and spent some time with him. Lou came in and was a lot better at helping, generally speaking, than I was.

One noon, I ate lunch downstairs in the lunchroom, and Mr. Monroe asked me over to their (Top Six) table, so we had an interesting conversation. I guess he's really not so bad. He lost his wife a year ago and is lonely. We walked upstairs to pick up our checks together, and he said he enjoyed the raised eyebrows!

Don offered to let me spend the night with *him*, if I ever get stranded again! Ha!

Mark came in to loan me a magazine I'd been interested in. He seems like such a sweet guy, same as most of the cadre. Yes, I guess maybe I *have* been "conned!"

I went through Six Block while the men were taking showers, but kept my blinders on.

Events of the week of February 9th

This was a fantastically busy week. I realize I'm a pushover for anyone who wants to stop in, and a lot do. There was a young guy--- pretty manic and completely amoral, as far as I could determine. He's been keeping the psychs busy, as he is all concerned over his placement, his appeal, and his love life.

Dr. C. has been dropping in, also Ethan. Since Don and I are on good terms again, maybe Ethan wonders what's up. Dr. C. asked me to critique a paper he wrote on systematizing group therapy. It took me quite a while to do that, evenings at home. I had spoken with him about my thesis study and its subsequent publication in the Journal of Clinical Psychology. He tells me he mentioned it to Houseworth and the Superintendent, and recommended that I be allowed to continue my work. He said they seemed impressed!

I've been doing parole evaluations, always with two other staff on the team. I do hate doing them. It takes me so long to dictate one, and it's such a responsibility. I worked on one at home for three hours. I don't like working with Owen. He gives each man the third degree and comes across as really pompous. I disagreed with him and Dr. C. on two.

Our hall porter in the bubble is a very surly-appearing black man who never speaks to any of us. I usually speak to him anyway. This week I noticed a lovely, hand-painted valentine on the bulletin board in the bubble. It was to R&GC staff, and had a beautiful sentiment and philosophy inside. It said, "From Charlie." He was sitting at the end of the hall, so I went over and we talked about his artwork and writing, I told him how much I appreciated what he had done! So--- he *can* talk. I was really touched. I told the guys about it at noon, and they just joked it off.

I dealt with an emergency, and told the group that I was feeling low about it, at lunch. Owen said, "Why? I *like* to make them cry!" Hmmm.

I went to the Muskegon Training Unit on Thursday with Don, Bob, and Dr. C. We stopped at Elias' in Lansing for coffee, and had a good time on the way over. We ate with their staff at a pizza place, and then took a tour with a Mr. Loveless. What a wonderful place to do time, if you have to, that is! It is new and very impressive. The land is wooded, the main rooms are carpeted, there is color TV, and up-to-the-minute everything. But there isn't enough for the men to do to keep them occupied. We didn't leave until 2:10, but believe it or not, Don made it back to Jackson by 4:30 so I could car pool home with Ronald. Paul is now working only three days a week.

Figure 17 - This card was in my Seven Block mailbox--- it seemed appropriate when I reviewed the files of the men I was to interview for my sex offender therapy group!

I interviewed more men for my group one day. There was Larry, who wants to switch groups (he's a mandatory lifer), and a black fellow who needs therapy to be considered for parole. There was also a very "flakey" young guy with a broken leg. Three men didn't even show up! But one black man came in when I was alone, just as though he belonged there--- but he didn't, and he began leering at me and coming toward me! He was between me and the door, so I couldn't get out! Luckily (?) just then another man came in to complain about the parole board, (or so he said!) and the other man departed in a hurry! In fact, both of them did, even before I could thank the second man. I can see I'll have to keep locking and unlocking the radio room door, as I was feeling pretty scared, and probably rightly so! I get shaky when I think about what could have happened.

I've been eating out in front with the guys lately. I tried carrying my purse inside on the way to a staff meeting, and it had a cinnamon roll in it left over from lunch. But no. The roll was confiscated during the search at the main gate! Incidentally, the food is even worse at the OD lately.

I sat in on Frank's group on Friday. They are a very sophisticated bunch and I didn't say very much. I had missed Frank by the time clock so I had to go up those dreaded stairs to the Academic School all by myself. I made it all right, I am thankful to report!

Events of the week of February 16th

Actually, Monday was a holiday, and I stayed home Friday with a stomach upset (food in the OD, maybe?). So there are only three work days to report about.

Jimmy seems quite distant, maybe because I stopped having lunch out front for a while, and have been eating up in the OD. I resisted the liver, however! I was on classification one day with Don. Most of the staff is in training, and I hear it is going well. I wonder when we will be getting another female on the staff. I've been around here for four months! Ronald says that besides the fact that he likes me personally, I'm one of the most valuable staff members--- dependable, and so on. Sometimes I don't feel that way, especially when I still make mistakes.

I sat in on Lou's sex offender group one afternoon. On the way, he showed me around both yards. There were plenty of stares! The meeting was in a building in the yard. About ten minutes after it began, two officers burst through the door. They were all upset about a lady being out there! I told them I was perfectly all right. The men in the group gave me a rough time during group with their questions. "How does a woman feel----?" etc. I tried to get across that

120

I couldn't speak for *all* women. It is really an event I'll remember, spending an hour and a half with a dozen rapists! They seem to fit into two categories. There is the hedonistic, sociopathic type, and then there is the neurotic who really hates himself. At the end of the group, one man wound it up by saying, "Now if you'll just leave your address and phone number, we'll all look you up when we're released!"

I received a kite from one man I OK'd for my group. It was pretty incoherent. I wonder if it will be possible to do therapy with him that way.

George Bowman called from Top Six. He wants me to see the man I referred up there when I first started work, which started so much controversy. Does this signify a truce, maybe?

I hear from the training group people that the officers really resent us psychs. What else is new?

Events of the week of February 23rd

During the first part of the week, most of the crew were in training, and the rest of us held the fort. Conditions are terrible. Over-crowded, dirty--- I have to push through crowds of men in the morning to get to my office. There were many catcalls and insolent remarks, the first of the week, but few toward the end. It's just an interesting, unexplained fact. I've been seeing six men every day with the exception of the morning that I was on classification. Steve said he chose me. Bill was supposed to do it but Steve needed someone fast. We went through seeing *60* men by noon! Steve took me downtown to lunch as a reward, even though I *had* become confused, a few times.

Wednesday I was duty therapist in the afternoon. I saw two men. One "old" man (he looked 65 but was actually 43) wouldn't come out of his cell or eat, and Officer Sanders was concerned. The man was confused and as paranoid as all get-out! They have him top-locked. I went up to his cell, and after we talked for a few minutes, I asked the man if he'd be willing to eat for *me*, because I'm concerned about him, and he said he would, "for the lady." I asked Sanders the next day, and yes, he's been eating!

Steve also sent a young man down from security classification. He had been top-locked because of a reported suicide attempt in county jail. He was smiling and congenial, and denied the suicide report. So I asked him about any suicide attempt, and he told me, sure, he and three friends had had a suicide pact, and so on. So I started asking about his offense. He said very cheerfully that he'd killed a girl. And also that he had seen psychiatrists, because he had burned her. "Why?" "I don't know." So I told him he'd continue top-locked and that I'd read his file. I took him back to Steve and Danny Elliottson, who'd been going to release him from top-lock! I got a look at the file the next morning and almost got sick. There was a lot of arson, drugs, suicide attempts, overt homosexual activity. Then he had started fires in the room where the girl was, and locked her in, to burn up. No one could get to her, and she was barely alive when the firemen broke in. I saw all the gory descriptions. I told Steve that I felt the man was an example of a schizophrenic with bizarre behavior and inappropriate affect--- an off-the-cuff diagnosis!

One day, I was done with six by 3:15. I received my rating from Ronald. A quality report, he put it, and it surely was. Unfortunately, he and Paul had a blowup, so Paul has decided not to carpool with us any more, and Ronald is relieved. I left Paul a note--- "*I* still love ya." He had kept us waiting half an hour after work while he talked with a suicide (attempt) in Top Six, and Ronald and I had no idea where he was.

I spent the week on Seven Block and was VERY busy. I went out to the lunchroom with Edward and Jimmy, then right back to work. I had felt that Jimmy has been distant lately, so I went to his office and asked him to tell me if he was angry, so I could either apologize, or tell him to go to hell! He said the only thing he doesn't like about me is that I'm paranoid, imagining that people don' like me, but that he realizes I'm working on this problem, and for goodness sake, *why* would I think that he, of all people, didn't like me??

I saw one man who had just found out he had a new son—and another I happened to interview on his birthday, and we celebrated a bit, about that. Another man was quite sullen and hostile, but came back as he was leaving and said, "I want you to know that you're really good at what you do." Another told me, "I wish there were more nice people like you around here." I also get more "black handshakes" lately. One boy ran in to tell me goodbye the day he rode out,

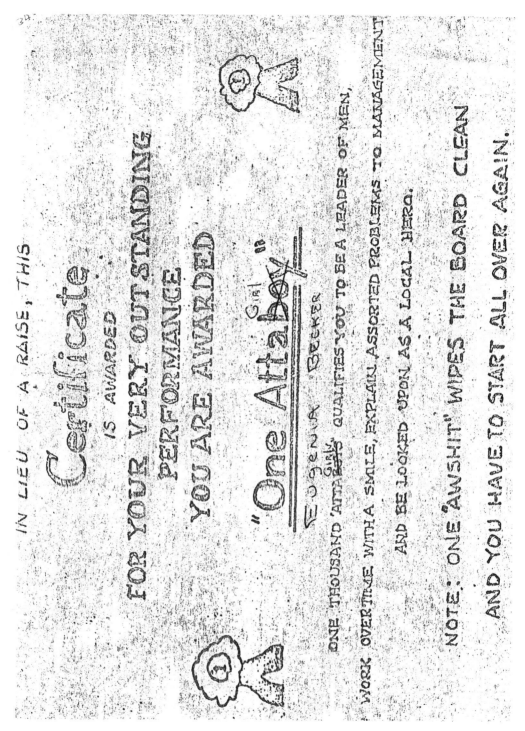

Figure 18 - A day brightener found in my mailbox.

and thanked me. I know, I know, it's a prison, never trust an inmate--- but does it do any harm to treat them as though they are still human beings?

Prentis tells us a resident friend of his says that "something's coming down." this summer, and that Ethan is on the list of people to *get*. For almost the first time since the first week of work, I really, really feel afraid. But I believe that the worst thing to do around here is to appear fearful, so I walk confidently and continue to smile and greet those who speak to me politely.

I did parole evaluations all day Tuesday at Trusty. In the morning I was with Owen and Dan. I am trying, not too successfully, not to dislike Owen! He is negative and hostile to the residents, puts me down, and takes over any situation. He seems very conceited. We saw one man who is in for raping his daughters, from age eight--- alternately, by nights. He had no remorse, only self-pity and denial. I joined Owen in negativity on that one!

Ronald and Paul had it out again. Paul came back to the carpool Monday and Ronald didn't explode until on the way home. He told Paul he doesn't like him and doesn't want him to ride with us. Paul came to my office during the day, to thank me for the note, and we talked for a while. He implied the problem could be jealousy. I didn't follow up on that, and now I really wonder what he meant. Professional jealousy? And both Ronald and Paul have girlfriends--- in fact, I've met the *two* who live with Ronald!

Cowboy came bouncing into my office to ask me if I'm older than thirty-seven. I told him "Yes" after he explained he had a bet on. He said he was sure I wasn't--- he's forty-one. I told him he is still young! He went out scratching his head and told me, "You sure take good care of yourself!"

I found myself really afraid of one man I interviewed. He is a sexual psychopath who raped his mother and five year old sister--- and stalked and raped an eleven year old. He sat there working his hand on his knee and I sure cut the interview short!

I also had quite a lengthy session with another black kid. He burst into my office without being called. I sent him back out twice, and I could hear him laughing outside my door. When I did call him in, it was a battle of wits--- and wills. I found we were playing all kinds of games. He is a *very* disturbed boy (age

20) and is serving two life sentences, one for rape. He was manipulative, threatening, insolent, and demanding. Someone had recommended psychotherapy for him before, and of course, he never got it. By the time he left, we had established some kind of rapport, I felt, and he told me he would appreciate it if I could get some help for him. However, Friday, another black man came in to tell me about "unsavory events" that had occurred the night before. And then the desk also called. It seems the young guy had got out of his cell and raped a white kid, and is now an inhabitant of Five West. What a shame! I wonder if I could have done more.

My dictionary seems to have become a status symbol. I loaned it to the man who brought me the message about the "night's events," and he strutted around with it sticking out of his pocket for two days! Just as soon as he returned it, another guy asked to borrow it. But I have learned my lesson--- loaning things to residents is *not* a good idea, and is probably against the rules as well!

I also managed to make Edward angry. He was "called on the carpet" by Ronald, for using an afternoon to teach the Rorschach and TAT (psychological tests) to others on the staff. I happened to be there, and found that very "far out," as I had studied the Rorschach for a full year in graduate school, and consider myself only a *beginner* in interpreting that complex test. So I had made a comment to that effect, which Ronald picked up on. I found it was a good idea to apologize, later, as Edward said it really burned him up. I should keep remembering that he has the Ph. D. and I am only a Master's level psychologist!

I spent more time in Trusty also, this week, interviewing the men in the Janitor's closet again! And I was in the subhall radio room one day, interviewing men for my group. I don't know why it is called the "radio room," as it's just a ramshackle room that looks largely unused. It is dirty, and one of the windows is broken, meaning that it is too cold in the winter and too hot in the summer (it faces south). There is one desk, in worse shape than the one in my office, and a number of straight chairs in various stages of disrepair. It is here that we are expected to be proficient enough as therapists, to prepare our group men for a return to society outside the walls, hopefully cured of whatever mental illness that has afflicted them! I did line up seven or eight men, the day I was there. I didn't feel well at all, that day--- was shaky, headachy, light headed. So Steve suggested I go to his house (a lot closer than going home would be!) and rest for a while. I gratefully accepted, as Don said it was OK, but after I got back, Don fussed when I punched out at regular time that night.

I went out to lunch on Friday with Dr. C. and Owen, of all people! It was the first nice day all week, as we have been having ice storms, wind storms, and severe rain storms.

Dan stopped in to see me Friday afternoon, ostensibly to ask questions about the MMPI (psychological test), which he administers as part of his job as a cadre clerk. While he was there, we got to visiting a bit, and it was good to get better acquainted. Just as he was leaving, he turned and said, "I want you to know you are always being observed." I wasn't sure at first how he meant it, because I realize everyone watches me through the small glass in my door. But he went on to say, "Nothing is going to happen to you while you're on Seven Block. People are watching to make sure--- even some clerks!" And he grinned and went out! I was really touched. I mentioned it to Ronald on the way home, and he said he'd been far behind me, as I walked out of the block, and noticed "Big John" (cadre) following about ten feet in back of me, all the way to the ramp. So I guess I have my own private bodyguard, at least when I'm on Seven Block.

Events of the week of March 8th

This week was really something else! And I had anticipated status quo while Don is away. It never happens! To begin with, I got myself into the most trouble with the "powers that be" since I've been working here! It all started because I've been receiving kites and innumerable drop-in visits from the man who borrowed my dictionary, Levon Johnson. When he comes in wanting to talk, he is polite, and comes across as a very intelligent, inquisitive, though probably disturbed young man, who really appreciates any attention I can give him. Some of his kites tell of his boyhood in a black neighborhood in Detroit, how he was caught up with the criminal behavior of his peers very early, and was first sentenced to prison when he was eighteen. He also speaks of his desire to become educated and it is clear that he spends a great deal of time trying to learn through reading. I wish I could help, but I did not do his intake interview and am not his therapist, so I have to cut his visits short in order to get my work done.

But when I was going through his many kites recently, it finally dawned on me that the handwriting and symbols he uses in them are the same as those in a rather threatening, unsigned note I received a while ago. So Tuesday after staff meeting, I talked with Bob about Levon. I told him that he has never been threatening to me in person, but some of the latest kites did sound quite sexual, and that the contents of some have convinced me that he is probably mentally ill. Well, Bob said he hadn't picked up on the psychosis until seeing the notes, but the manic hyperactivity he displays in the block was obvious to us both. So Bob came over to my office to read the letters, he felt that they were indeed a threat, and suggested we ask for top-lock for Mr. Johnson. I asked him to please, let me think it over, but I did give him the notes to take out to show to Ronald. It is very hard for me to know what to do. Some of the kites are lengthy--- five or six pages of pretty unintelligible rambling, but then one will arrive that is completely lucid, and asks my forgiveness for the others.

I feel that Levon may have become dependent on the contact he has with me to help him retain his last bit of sanity in this place. Bob said that Don had classified him to Marquette, which is not a place where he will receive any needed treatment. Bob felt that the classification to Marquette was pretty inappropriate, too. So after much thought, the next day I spoke with Ronald, Bob, and Steve to request that Levon be reclassified for two reasons; so that he could ride out sooner, and so he could do his time someplace where he could be treated, not punished. All of them felt it was a good idea, and I went up to classification and gave Steve Levon's number.

But as I was leaving for the day, Bob told me that now we have more trouble! They had found a note in Don's box (Don is still away) from Levon, just asking, "How's your daughter?!" As I reached GOS to punch out that night, Bob, Ronald and Steve were discussing it, and asked me how I felt about toplock for Levon now, and I knew I had to agree, as it all did sound pretty threatening. So they phoned and had Officer Smith take Levon up to toplock immediately. Then, while we were still down in the lunchroom, I learned that they intended to use Levon's notes to me in a security classification hearing against him. I asked if that was necessary, especially since Steve said he was classifying him to go inside SPSM, and I knew I might well run into Levon there in the future. They both said yes, it was necessary! I tried to argue, but could not prevail, and felt so helpless!

I told Steve I felt like throwing a tantrum, and he said, "Then I'd have to toplock *two* of you!" and he hugged me. But I was so upset, the tears kept starting again, all the way home. I was angry at Ronald at first, too, and didn't respond when he tried to explain.

I felt that both Levon and I were getting bad deals, though in different ways! Yes, he may prove to be dangerous, and yes, he is probably psychotic, and I should know by now, that if you are mentally ill and in prison, you can expect only minimal help or treatment at best, and are much more apt to face severe punishment instead. And now such an individual, who had come to me as someone he could turn to for help, will see me as the enemy for turning over his kites as evidence against him!

That night, I took a valium in order to sleep awhile, then I got up and typed out a protest stating that my property (Levon's kites) were being used without my permission, and that he had never been personally threatening to me. I showed it to Ronald, who disagreed with the part about the use of my kites, but said I should give it to Steve. So I took it up to Steve and he received it very coldly. Later, Bob dropped in (I'd given him a copy) and said Steve was really angry, and didn't even want to tell *him* where he was sending Levon, until Bob had demanded to know. Ionia, thank goodness, not SPSM. I felt a bit better, but still upset at the whole system!

Well, that night after work was a get-together at the Roadhouse for both Custodial and Treatment staff. On the way over, Ronald said he had something to tell me. He said it wasn't *too* bad, but that he'd wait until after he had a few beers, to tell me! So on the way home, he told me Steve had shown my note to the Superintendent who said he was upset with Ronald for allowing me to give it to Steve and that he wanted to talk with me. So--- sure enough, next morning the Superintendent called me into his office in the bubble. However, it was more to explain why Levon's kites were a threat, than to criticize me. It seems that some of the language in the kites was Black Muslim, and the gist was that I have a lot of black in me. I'm not sure what that means. I don't know that I should find that derogatory, but I can also see the concern. Anyway, Steve no longer seems angry, but says he IS going to use the letters. Then, of all things, I received another one--- and this one was a definite threat on Don's life. I debated what to do, and finally dumped it on Ronald. I surely do dread security classification day this week!

Figure 19 - My protest to Classification over their using Levon's kites against him.

Incidentally, there are lots of rumors going around. Riverside Center for classification of younger offenders is soon to open, so who is going?? The grapevine has it that Don will go to Lansing, Andy (the Superintendent) will be warden of SPSM, Jimmy will take Steve's place in classification--- and me? I will stay right where I am. Steve *is* moving up, to Lansing in about six weeks. I will miss him.

I interviewed two more potential group members. One was an alcoholic who murdered his wife, the second was a transvestite who attacks attractive women. They seemed pretty much OK and wanted to be in my group. Just as the second man was leaving, he said, "Say, you are an attractive woman. Mr. Griffith told me you were, and you *are* attractive!" I said, "Thanks very much--- be seeing you" and I tried not to appear to shove him out the door!

I went through the subhall and up to the OD alone twice this week. Jimmy and Edward seem somewhat distant, but no one is saying why. I feel badly about that.

There were more parole evaluations this week. I do like to read Owen's, and I told him they are excellent. (I give credit where credit is due!) He said he thinks his and mine are about the best. Ronald tells me mine are so consistently good that he rarely bothers to check them anymore.

I interviewed a man who murdered a hitchhiker with a ball-peen hammer, and an old man who shot his wife and left her in bed for three weeks. (He was a show producer, earning a six figure salary--- before he hit the skids.) Lastly, I did a parole evaluation on a man who had just been brought back as far as the bubble, from a Correction Center furlough by his parole officer. Edward and Jimmy and I took him over to the lunchroom--- and right in front of the guy, they both said they didn't want to interview him, and flipped a coin to see who had to. That was gross. No wonder the man was hostile and sullen when I interviewed him!

Friday, just as we arrived, they waved us away from the side entrance of the main building, which we use as a shortcut to get to the place where we punch in. They said there was a bomb in there! So we went to the front door of SPSM instead and from there, punched in as usual, but we did smell something hot. Later we learned that there WAS a bomb--- and it was lit, but they dragged it away from the building and later exploded it elsewhere. Every once in a while, you are reminded what a grim place this is!

At staff meeting, Frank voiced a lot of concern over ethics. These are things we all feel, and worry about, so it was pretty emotional. But Ethan cut Frank right down. What a hostile man! I've read his reports on men we had seen together, and just couldn't *believe* he and I were describing the same person!

MICHIGAN DEPARTMENT OF CORRECTIONS
RECEPTION & GUIDANCE CENTER
DIVISION OF PSYCHOLOGICAL SERVICES

PSYCHOLOGICAL REPORT

NAME	NUMBER	INTERVIEW DATE 4-11-78

OFFENSE Assault to Robbery Armed, Rape Parole Violator	TERM 5-10	AGE 38

TESTS ADMINISTERED:	☐ BETA, S.A.T., M.M.P.I., I.S.B., B.G., D.A.P., B.P.I., S.T.E.A. ☐ BETA, W.A.I.S., W.R.A., B.G., D.A.P., S.T.E.A. ☒ CLINICAL INTERVIEW ☒ OTHER: (PAROLE BOARD EVALUATION).

REASON FOR REFERRAL: A current psychological report has been requested by the Parole Board for purposes of assessing the subject's suitability for parole consideration.

PSYCHODYNAMICS: The reader is referred to the Psychological Report of 3-1-77 by Dr. _____. The details of behavior and the etiology of criminal behavior do not differ significantly from that which is recorded in that report. Nor did this clinician find any indications of psychosis or gross psychological impairment. It is noted that Mr. ___ has been identified as retarded with an IQ of 63. In behavioral terms this would indicate that Mr. ___ would have difficulty and be slower in grasping abstract terms. It does not mean that his intellectual limitations interfere with his ability to function in a normal society or interfere with his ability to be totally responsible for his own life.

The events of Mr. _____ s life are recorded in the report of 3-1-77. Mr. ___ s recitation of those events are essentially the same today as they were at that time, except this clinician found nothing that would indicate that Mr. ___ is consciously resentful of his mother. Quite the contrary, on a conscious level, Mr. ___ is very supportive to his mother stating that she was the only one that would come to his aid during the severe beatings by his father and was sympathetic to his position. That she wasn't a strong woman in the sense of being able to remove either herself or her child from the rather brutal attacks of the father is supposition as is the fact that she is promiscuous by the fact that she produced three children out of wedlock from three different fathers. However, the details do not change the fact that the home life of Mr. ___ in his developmental years was both characterized by gross instability, high incidence of violence, and in preadolescence replacing parental love with institutionalized living.

It also continues to be true of Mr. _____ that he denies culpability in sex crimes and attributes the cause for the other armed actions to be drugs and his use of alcohol. In short, we find a young man growing up in an environment in which he has limited intellectual resources but who is confronted with a very complex but basically negative socialization who at this point in time (38 years of age) has very little insight into the nature and causes of his behavior. It is further this clinician's opinion, that such insight in such intellectual processing of his behavior and understanding of its causes is very unlikely. In responding to the question as to what he had gained from his psychotherapeutic experience his responses were quite general and with very little risk involved. They tended to be a textbook answer rather than a demonstration of his own insights. Thus we have here an individual who not only has a good deal of anger and hostility for the way that he was raised and how he has related to adults but one who has been systematically exposed to violence and aggression as a viable means of resolving difficulties and problems. We also have an individual who is intellectually unable to process ethical considerations beyond third stage moral development, which is you do it because it is expected of you. Couple with this an individual who is impulsive, emotionally immature, has demonstrated very poor judgment capacities and you have the makings of a serious social problem. Add

Figure 20 - Above and following 2 pages — An adequate Parole Board Report, although the man's therapists added a few encouraging words on last page.

to this already explosive mixture, drugs and alcohol and it becomes uncontrollable.

The rather interesting thing in reading through Mr.   's material is that he apparently has done very well in the structured environment of prison. He has been recommended a number of times for special considerations for parole and has good to excellent work reports. In short Mr.   , has profited from a structured environment and has demonstrated that he can function within prescribed limits and fulfill the expectations of those who are his supervisors. The critical point demonstrated is that Mr.   has functioned well in a very structured environment. Mr.   's personal plan for parole is to get released, to get a job, to get married and raise a family and to become a member of society. As meritorious as those desires may be, they appear to be rather unrealistic in terms of Mr.   's background and the possible support that he would receive from his environment.

RECOMMENDATIONS: Mr.   is a 38 year old individual with limited intellectual functioning who was victimized as a child and exposed to violence, social instability and replaced parental love with institutionalization. He is currently emotionally immature, impulsive, limited decision making powers with some anger and hostility. He has limited insight into the causal factors in his behavior. He denies culpability in the sexual activity and projects blame upon drugs and alcohol for his assaultive behavior in robbery. In contrast he has functioned well within a highly structured environment to the point of warranting special recognition.

If parole is granted it appears necessary for Mr.   to design a parole circumstance that contains some of the structure that allowed him to work and function successfully in prison. Including definitive jobs, place of residence, free time activity. He should refrain from any act of aggression or assault. He should not use any alcohol or drugs. He should not involve himself in gambling or other street activities either as recreation or for remuneration. There should be frequent and regular reporting dates which are absolutely required. If parole is not granted, it is the recommendation of this clinician that Mr.   be placed in a Correction Center in which the preparations for parole might be made, including the finding of a job, the establishment of a place of residence and the development of a certain basic kind of structure which allows him to begin to assume more responsibility for himself. It is this clinician's opinion that psychotherapeutic services is of very little value to Mr.   due to the intellectual limitations and his socialization.

                                                            , Ph.D.
                                        Clinical Psychologist

                        Consultants: , Ph.D.
                                        Clinical Psychologist

4-11-78
JRP/vj   , Ph.D.
4-11-78   Chief Psychologist

Orig: Institutional Main File
  cc: Parole Board (2)   Jean Becker
       Counselor File   Jean Becker, M.A.
       Psychological Services   Clinical Psychologist

ADDENDUM:

Although we, as Mr.   's psychotherapists, are generally in agreement with the foregoing
report by Dr.   we wish to add the following statements of clarification--as well as
our professional/clinical opinion regarding specific issues wherein we do not agree.

We, too, disagree with Dr.   'n's (3-1-77) view that Mr.   's primary locus of anger
or hostility was his mother. Rather, we sense that he is much more emotionally and behav-
iorally involved, in a negative way, with his father. These dynamics also tend to generalize
to others in authority positions. Moreover, his present (as well as previous) sex offense
seems more related to his dramatic attempts to offset feelings of inadequacy as a man, than
hostility directed at females, per se. His assaultive history is also believed directly
related to strong "macho strivings" designed to compensate for his feelings of male inadequacy and to "strike back" at the world he perceived as rejecting and nonunderstanding of
his needs.

Mr.   has been involved in Group Psychotherapy for Sex Offenders, with the undersigned,
for approximately seven months, with an excellent attendance and participation record.
Contrary to Dr.   's belief, we feel that this resident has made therapeutic progress.
While it is certainly true that Mr.   has not fully accepted responsibility for his
sexual acting out (he steadfastly claims the victim was a willing sex partner until the
appearance of her boyfriend, whereupon she screamed "rape"), he has shown some good therapeutic gains. For example, he has gained insight into the dynamics of his feelings of
inadequacy and alienation, and is in the process of learning to respond in more constructive
ways. Also, he has become more adept in interpersonal communications--especially with
females via the female co-therapist. Finally, he has demonstrated an improved decision-
making process/capability in dealing with significant others in his home environment. Thus,
although Mr.   has not resolved all of his difficulties, we believe he is demonstrating
progress in the above mentioned areas.

                                                            , Ph.D.
                                          Psychotherapist

                                          Jean Becker, M.A.
                                          Psychotherapist

4-20-78
JVR/vj
4-26-78

The drinking bout at the Roadhouse that night was sort of a bust, by the
way. Only three of the custody staff showed up. But I had a good talk with Bob,
anyway. He does seem to be the one person who understands why I felt asI did
about the way Levon's case was handled, even though he thinks I was wrong in
minimizing the danger. And he's probably right.

I'm glad this week is over, not that it was awful, or anything. I just felt glum over a lot of things. First of all, Ronald received a letter via the Superintendent, from Six Block, requesting that I not walk through the block any more. It upsets the residents! Now I will have a trek outside in order to go anywhere in the prison from Seven Block (except the yard or maybe Eight Block)! Evidently, Don neglected to tell me about this earlier. And the subhall door guard stopped me because I had no escort. And Ronald was really snappish in the car, and says I told too many people too much, concerning the Levon Johnson case.

The end of this week I'll have been here five months! Next week is a vacation, of sorts. I am to go to "New Employee's Orientation," along with Edward.

I also did a bunch of parole evaluations, which I still hate to do. On Wednesday, when coming back to the block with Dr. C. and Lou, Lou stopped in Classification to see Steve. As I was waiting on the gallery for him, I heard a voice say, "Oh, Mrs. Becker"--- and I turned and saw Levon!! I had picked up a bunch of kites that were stuck in my door and that I hadn't yet read, and he told me that they were his. Then he assured me that he was fine, and was going inside Jackson! I told him it was good to talk with him again, and I wished him well. As I turned to go, he asked if I'd had any *trouble* recently, in a rather strange way. I kept going, and began reading his kites in Lou's office. They varied from downright sexual to a very rational explanation of why he dislikes Don. I felt suddenly really scared and shaky, and asked Lou if he'd walk me down the stairs to my office, and off the block at 4:15. And he did, but Levon was gone by then. I ran into Jimmy in the lobby--- he'd been on Security Classification--- and he asked if I was OK. I guess I looked awful. We went down to the lunchroom to talk briefly. He did *not* read Levon's letters that had been written to me, during the hearing, and so he had just classified Levon to SPSM! Apparently, his classification to Ionia was predicated on his being a threat to women--- and they needed to use my letters for that! What a tangled web---

Friday I had pretty well recovered from this, when, as I was returning from getting my mail at Grier's office, I saw Levon by my office door waiting to see me! I gulped and invited him in. Fortunately, he was friendly and polite, as usual. He talked about the symbolism of a dead roach in one of the kites he had sent to Don. He was aware that I had asked not to have my kites read, and he thanked me. I felt good about that. I can only hope that somehow, he will make it through his sentence and come out intact, but I doubt if this progressive system of ours will be of much assistance.

I sort of enjoyed the contact I had with some of the young kids I had to see toward the last of the week. Sometimes I feel I can reach them---

I went out to lunch with Edward and Jimmy, but I didn't feel wanted. I guess I'll plan not to see them as much, from now on.

One day I got a lecture from Steve about my being too emotionally involved with the problems of the men I see. Um hmm. It certainly seems that no one else is! Steve says he is leaving for Camp Baraga in the Upper Peninsula. I like Steve a lot, but we surely see things differently.

Oh yes, one day I asked Edward to see one man in my stead, as he was a sexual psychopath, rapist and exposer, and was considered unpredictable. But the man himself barged into my office to see *me*, just as nurse Wilkinmaster was leaving. Wilkinmaster had come in to ask if I would talk with the man, "Please!" as he'd been troublesome the night before. I said I would, and I did, but I got him out of there fast when he asked me if males and females were different, and if women can do things with their bodies that men can't! He also complained of pain all over and a cyst under his testicles. Incidentally, the man is about seven feet tall! I called Bishop on Top Six and said I was sending the man up. The next day Bishop called back and we had a nice chat. He says he hates the bad feelings between our two units and hopes to break the ice. Great! Rumor has it, though, that CSU will be leaving Top Six soon, as part of a reorganization, and that PSU may inherit their quarters!

Events of the week of March 22nd

Edward and I were in new employee training all week. It was quite an experience! We spent two days walking all over SPSM--- on the roof, up gun turrets, through the industries, the auditorium, the drug company buildings where they test new drugs on prisoners who volunteer, the vocational school, the Big Top (dining hall), the arsenal, just about the whole area inside the walls-- they even came to R&GC. Other days we saw films and video tapes. The 1952 riot was impressive and very chilling. (What am I doing in a place like this?? Sigh. Just a rhetorical question!)

I received two "Thank you" kites in one day! Now there is no lack of kites to read. I also found myself discussing Levon's case with Don, who is back, but I never should have. He suggested I go to Five Block to see him, if I'm that concerned! Actually, I did try once to see a man who was in Five Block. I asked the officer at the desk in the Rotunda politely. He looked at me as though I was crazy and gave me a stone cold "NO." Apparently Don had Levon taken there, as soon as he returned after being off work. Five West is "The Hole" and I hear it is a terrible, degrading place, especially for someone whose sanity is precarious at best. I consulted with Bob, and asked a big favor of him--- to go over to Five Block and check on Levon for me. He did, and reported that he found him lying there in a cell, naked and unresponsive.

What a great disservice the state did when they closed the mental hospitals, and shifted the responsibility of caring for the mentally ill largely to the Department of Corrections! I realize now that there is really almost nothing I can do to help this man, and the tragedy is that Levon's case can be multiplied by the thousands, as the mentally ill keep arriving, and continue to be punished, not treated.

Oh, Adam Rothschild from CSU is to take Don's place as Administrator of Psychological Services. Everyone is very concerned--- except Ethan. We had a staff meeting Friday afternoon, and Ethan said he feels we (not he!) need more supervision, because of our poor reports!

I saw one of Frank's group members in the Trusty kitchen during training, and he let loose with a hostile barrage at all of us. I have no idea why!

There are 57 1/2 acres inside the walls of SPSM, and the walls are 35 feet high. We walked all over this week, followed by two officers with a walkie-talkie and a man on the roof with a rifle. While we were on the infirmary elevator, one resident was so angry he could hardly restrain himself! I only heard remarks from one man aimed directly at me, though, and that was in the subhall. They are saying women can't eat in the OD any more, but so far I'm getting in. Though now that Six Block is off limits, I have to go all the way out of Seven Block and up the ramp after it is unlocked, and out of the bubble into the fresh air and walk 300 feet or so to enter the main building. There, I must go through both main gates to get to the rotunda and eventually, to the subhall and the OD. I must take the same route to get to my therapy groups in the radio room.

Notes written May 21st

There hasn't been a dull day since I wrote last, but some recent events seem more worth writing about than most. As of now, I've been working here for seven months, and received a favorable 6 month's rating. I have gone to the next step, pay-wise, and Don, in preparation for his leaving, wrote a very complimentary letter for the file. Now it looks as though he won't be leaving us until this fall, however.

After I last wrote, I began receiving kites from Levon again, first from Five Block, and then (finally) from Top Six. His description of life in Five West bore out what I already surmised when I was not allowed admission. It is not just segregation, but certain punishment, for those who are sent there. Levon complained that occupants of Five West are allowed only one shower a week, and that he had forfeited even his much anticipated weekly cleansing, because of some infraction he didn't understand. He also mentioned that he had been called "Nigger" three times by staff, thus far. His notes from Top Six are somewhat less descriptive of his circumstances and are also less coherent. However, in one kite he states, probably correctly, "You are the only person in this institution who cares at all what happens to me." Somehow, Levon's case always brings home to me how little power I have to make any real difference in the treatment of individuals I encounter here.

Other events of interest since I last wrote--- Bob asked me to co-author some research with him, on predicting violence. I felt really pleased and flattered that he chose me. Dr. C., as head of the Research Committee, gave his approval, and so did Don. Then at our first staff colloquium, Rothschild put us all down, and said no time will be available for research and called our staff "Mickey Mouse." He also put down Frank, who was doing a presentation on therapy. So Bob and I got together and composed a memo to Don saying we were quitting our research, and exactly why. Not long after, Don came down to my office. He'd taken the memo to Andy, who'd called Rothschild on the carpet, with Don present. The upshot of it was that Rothschild actually apologized, to me and to Bob. But even that was a put-down to me, since he managed to address all of his comments, except a criticism of one of my reports, to Bob! But we are going back at it, at our own pace. Bob and I are good friends, now, and enjoy working together. We seem to feel the same about so many things.

Next item! Todd, Harry, Lou and I all took the GATB (General Aptitude Test Battery) one day. This is a test given to all the residents when they enter, to establish their capabilities in a number of areas, and is very helpful in determining what kinds of programs (scholastic or trade) they would be most suited for. They felt it would be good for us to see what the men have to go through before we interview them. It took us all morning. Well, later Todd gave me the computerized scores, and it seems I scored highest overall, with General IQ 150, verbal, 165, high on all skills but two, as I fell down to average or below on finger dexterity and clerical. Todd summarized our results for staff at the next colloquium, which was embarrassing!

I also gave my talk on "Depression, all you never wanted to know!" for the staff, based on my research publication. It took an hour and a quarter, and seemed to go well. Don kept asking questions, and Ethan disagreed (of course!) He has a different view, based on the medical (psychiatric) model of mental illness. It just so happened that the same day, the prison had a general mobilization, with all the sirens going off and officers scrambling! I was in classification with Jimmy, and proceeded right away to Seven Block desk with him. Lights were flashing, men running, officers yelling, cells banging closed--- This was just at lunch when the men were eating. There were many curses and hoots, as they were hustled back to their cells. I sat on the bench and watched awhile, and then Captain Steuben beckoned to me to follow, and he let me out via the ramp to the bubble. I appreciated that, and was glad to go, because I was hungry as well as worried! Eventually, it got dull in the visitor's waiting room (near the main lobby). I watched the rifle squad march through, talked with Milt, and attempted rather unsuccessfully to strike up a conversation with Dr. Mannion, the new psychiatrist who, it is rumored, is to be in charge of all us mental health

WILLIAM G. MILLIKEN, GOVERNOR

DEPARTMENT OF CORRECTIONS

PERRY JOHNSON, Director

State Prison of Southern Michigan
4000 Cooper Street
Jackson, Michigan 49201

April 29, 1976

To Whom It May Concern

Ms. Eugenia Becker came to the Psychological Services Unit in an unusual status. She is the first female psychologist to work specifically in the Reception and Guidance Center quarantine facility. She is only the second woman to be employed in 7-Block at all. I have been particularly impressed with Ms. Becker's ability to come into a traditionally male professional setting and exercise the virtues of composure, common sense, and an unerring pursuit of a dignified professional role in the face of the inevitable pressures and resistance that fundamental change can bring to an organization. She has acquitted herself well and I feel she has distinguished herself as a valuable member of the professional team in the Psychological Services Unit. I should like to commend her for her outstanding performance and want to encourage her to continue the pursuit of a career in corrections. She has already rendered a valuable service to both the unit and the Department of Corrections as well as the field of corrections in general by helping to blaze the way for additional females to be integrated into our staff.

Sincerely,

D. E. Houseworth, Ph.D.
Administrator
Psychological Services Unit
Reception and Guidance Center

DEH/dmc

cc:

_____, Ph.D.
E. Becker
File

Figure 21 - Kudos from Dr. Houseworth after 6 months were appreciated.

folks. Finally, I went back to the bubble and sat there until the lockdown was over. They had cleared everyone out, shooed visitors away, and so on. I hope it is never for real!

Anyway, the lockdown put me far behind in my work, and I didn't catch up for days. Usually, I can count on Lou to help out, though. He can do men at a terrific rate, but most often his reports are, well, *short!* (I'm being kind!) Oh, I have captured second place in number of men seen--- behind Lou, of course!

My group, presently with Ronald, is surprising me. We have been meeting for about five weeks. Ronald was gone one of the first weeks, and it went OK without him. I'm no powerhouse therapist, but the men seem to like me--- Greg, Joe, Benny, John, Reggie, Thad, Joe, Bob, and sometimes Danny and Tom. I've had to send word to Joe that he's being dropped, though. All he wants is a clearance for furloughs. Greg is a brain and very passive aggressive, but does seem to be feeling a lot. Joe had resolved to keep still, but couldn't--- Once, he was so threatened, he closed us all out for a time, with no contact. But the next week, the depression had lifted and elation had set in. He came to me after group and told me that if I keep one important quality, caring, that I'll make a top-notch therapist. He said the rest of the group had pointed out to him that I really do care. Well, I really do---about most of them. Ronald says my group has developed trust very fast and he's amazed. Me too!

I stopped in at Bob's office the day of Rothchild's tirade, and Frank was there. I started to leave, and Bob asked me to sit down. He told me that Ronald, Frank, and he had been working on a proposal for a big project, a new experimental living unit, designed to test what therapies *work*, and would I be willing to help out? It might be one way (maybe) to get out from under Adam Rothschild's direction. I felt really flattered once again, and accepted, of course. We all met in Ronald's office another day and I was asked to be in charge of the testing. I'm working now on my part of the proposal--- which is top secret.

Also, Ronald and I both spoke to Andy (the Superintendent) about the possibility of our transferring to Riverside, when a reception center opens there. He said "fine" and so did Don. Also, Bob had decided, even before that, that he'd be going, so now the three of us are in it together. Don says he has plans for me, Dr. C. and Bob, to work with him in the future. Great! But--- Ronald has been asked to begin work at Clinical Services Unit *soon,* and Bob also. They hope to insist on my coming along, too. I'm not too happy about the prospect of working up there, but I want to get out from under Adam Rothschild and stay with Bob and Ronald. But Riverside is also turning out to be a "frying pan into the fire," deal. Dr. Mannion spoke to us one day and told of his plans. All the money and resources will be used to poke shots into 300 psychotics, and all the rest of the work (with no extra help) would go to us at the Psychological Services Unit! Don told him that it was "shit," but Mannion never blinked an eye. Psychologists are just lackeys, to him, apparently.

Dr. C. has asked me to publish my paper in his new Corrections Department Journal, help him edit the journal, and said if I want to go on with my depression research, he'd like to co-author. However, Bob and I have lost some of our faith in him, even though he is up for the Nobel Prize, and spent last weekend with Margaret Mead! He never makes an attempt to stand up for us, but does manage to take credit for many good things. I really wonder---

Well, a new female psych is coming soon, we are told. I hope so! Of course, the guys are all excited!

I took some self-defense training, as part of the new employee course. I really did well and enjoyed it. I thought I might *need* it Thursday. I was relieving Earl during the noon hour. An older black man came in and wanted to talk with a psych. I said at one o'clock, I could see him in my office for a few minutes. But he came back before one, just as Willy, the clerk, was leaving. The man closed the office door, sat down, and exposed himself!! I climbed around him to the door, after warning him to stop to no avail, and found Todd and Dan in the next office. I told them what had happened, and then things began--- It looked as though the National Guard was arriving! The guy was led away handcuffed. Lt. Miller instructed me to write out a ticket. And on my own, I also wrote a referral to Top Six. Dan suggested I give one of my afternoon men to Lou, so I did, as I was just a bit shaken. Anyway, George Bowman informed me the next day that it's being prosecuted as a *felony!* I certainly didn't anticipate that, as I felt the man surely had mental problems. Word got around fast! Deemer came in and asked Edward to leave. He told me he and Ty and some of the others have determined to protect me, and will always be watching out for me. He said they think I'm a nice person and felt badly for me. Bless them--- I have so many good friends! Cowboy came to me and apologized, too. He said if he'd been there, there'd have been nothing left of the guy to lock up!

Some of the residents I've seen recently have been fascinating. One depraved, 65 year old sex offender has been molesting young girls since he got his ten year old sister pregnant, when he was a teen! His latest victim was only three years old. He made obscene remarks to my face in the cell block. Another man was *very* hostile, no cooperation at all, just pure fury. It was a bit hard to deal with.

I've done a lot of parole evaluations, too. A few of the men are quite upset, but I'm honest with them and tell them what I am going to write, so far!

Everyone predicts riots, even the underground newspaper.

Steve is already gone, to Baraga, and Jimmy's suffering through Steve's job doing classification, temporarily. He told us that his wife had their baby--- congratulations, Jimmy!

Walsh Advances

Walsh came to the department in 1974 as a clinical psychologist and outpatient coordinator at the Reception and Guidance Center, a position he held until being named chief psychologist.

Previously he was employed for the Michigan Division of Vocational Rehabilitation as an quality assurance examiner in its disability program. He also was project assistant for the Rehabilitation Research and Training Center in Mental Retardation at the University of Wisconsin.

From 1968 to 1971 he was a disability examiner and vocational specialist for the Michigan Division of Vocational Rehabilitation.

He earned his doctor's degree in 1975 and his master's in 1971 from the University of Wisconsin.

Robert Walsh, Ph. D.

Figure 22 - Dr. Robert Walsh becomes Chief Psychologist of the Psychological Services Unit.

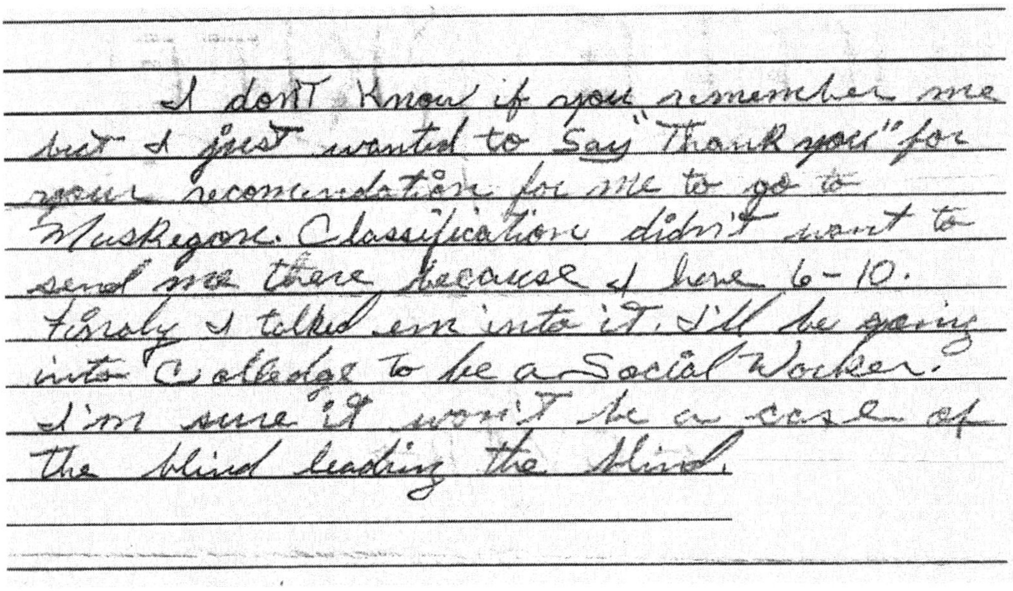

I don't know if you remember me but I just wanted to say "Thank you" for your recomendation for me to go to Muskegon. Classification didn't want to send me there because I have 6-10. Finaly I talked em into it. I'll be going into Colledge to be a Social Worker. I'm sure it won't be a case of the blind leading the blind.

Figure 23 - An encouraging kite.

1977

Well, I had good intentions! First I wrote in my journal every day, then every week, and lastly, every month. Now a long time has passed, more than a year, actually. I'm not sure how well I can reconstruct all that has happened from my brief notes, since that last entry, but it does seem as though it is still important to keep some kind of a record of all that has been going on.

This has been a period when change almost became commonplace! And this is true for me especially, on a personal level. As I mentioned before, because we both have backgrounds in research, Bob and I had begun working together on various projects, and then to our surprise (and everyone else's as well) we realized we had fallen in love! I am waiting for a divorce, (an amiable split-up, I am glad to say), and in the meantime, I am living in Jackson, where Bob and I can be together. Since we began here in 1975, when Bob and I were just co-workers, Bob's talents and education (Ph.D.) have been recognized and rewarded. First he was assigned by Don to take over Ronald's job when Ronald suddenly resigned to take work elsewhere, and then recently, he advanced to Don's old position as Administrator of Psychological Services, when Don went up the career ladder to a position in Lansing Office.

One thing hasn't changed, though--- I am still here, working in Seven Block. But I'm not a "fish" any longer, and have gained a bit of status in the past year or so. I've been reallocated several times already, due to recommendations from the powers that be, past and present, here in Psychological Services. Actually, I have gone as far as I can go here without a Ph.D.

I was put in charge of the training of all new employees in our unit for their first two weeks, not long after I last wrote, and this is something I enjoy, as I have a chance to get to know each one. The training that I had received, I felt had been haphazard at best, so I began putting together a training manual that new staff could consult. The manual early on was fairly manageable, at several hundred pages. However, the Department of Corrections is certainly good at one

TO: Mr. Ray Kraft, Personnel Officer
State Prison of Southern Michigan

DATE: December 13, 1976

FROM: , Ph.D., Administrator
Psychological Services Unit, R&GC

JBJECT: Reallocation request for Ms. Eugenia Becker

Upon assuming my position as Administrator of the Psychological Services Unit during a routine review of all Reception Center personnel I reviewed Ms. Becker's performance and classification level. She initially was hired as a Psychologist Trainee 08 in October of 1975. By definition the Psychologist Trainee 08 positions are automatically reallocated to 09 positions after one year of service unless the employee is separated. Upon examining the experience and educational requirements for the Psychologist 09 and 10 levels, I found that Ms. Becker should have initially been employed as a Psychologist 09 which would qualify her for a promotion to a 10 level after one year. Thq qualifications for a Psychologist 09 are "one year experience in psychology, and possession of a Masters' Degree in Psychology of equivalent graduate school credit toward a doctoral degree in Psychology (30 semester hours)." The qualifications for the Psychologist 10 are "two years experience in Psychology, one year of which shall have been subsequent to the obtaining of a Masters' degree in Psychology; and possession of a Masters' degree in Psychology or equivalent graduate school credit toward a doctor's degree in Psychology (30 semester hours)." Also there is indication that the Psychologist 10 is expected to have "greater skill and application of the knowledge and abilities required at the lower level."

Upon examining Ms. Becker's education experience, I found the following:

1. Education -

    A. Lansing Community College graduate with AA Degree Suma Cum Laude 1969 with a class standing of Valedictorian.
    B. Michigan State University graduate with BA Degree with high honors in 1971 with a class standing of upper 2 percent.
    C. Central Michigan University graduate with Masters' Degree in Clinical Psychology (two year program) in 1973 with an "A" average.

2. Clinical Internship - Winter 1972-73 at Midland/Gladwin Community Mental Health Center, Midland, Michigan.

    Also her Central Michigan training provided her with training in projective techniques (Rorschach, T.A.T., W.I.S.C., W.A.I.S., M.M.P.I., House-Tree-Person, 16 P.F., Stanford Benet, Q-Sort) along with specialty training in personality growth groups, psychodrama groups, substance abuse programming, rational and emotional therapy, and empathy and sexuality skills.

3. Full Time Work Experience - October, 1975 to present - Psychologist - Reception and Guidance Center, Michigan Department of Corrections. In this position Ms. Becker serves as a professional psychologist and renders psychological, educational, vocational and intelligence tests. Administers projective techniques, conducts psychotherapy with personality disorders and psychotics, prepares clear and concise psychological evaluations, and displays tact and professional expertise to function as an independent health professional.

Figure 24 - Above and following 2 pages – The new administrator's effort to get me a raise in status--- and pay! See pay stub on third page.

146

May, 1974 - June, 1975 - Information Evaluation Systems, Michigan
Department of Social Services. In this capacity her job duties were to
evaluate reports requested by the Probate Court and Department of Social
Services on delinquent juveniles. Reports contained psychological and
sociological analysis which requires knowledge of statistical techniques
used in study of behavior, a knowledge of emotional, social, psychological
and environmental problems, along with a knowledge and principals and
practices of clinical psychology and abnormal psychology with an ability
to relate her findings to professional personnel.

4. Part Time Employment - February, 1974 - May, 1974 - 20 hours per week -
    Assistant Director of Common Ground Crisis Center - St. Johns, Michigan.
    In this capacity her position required her to supervise and train peer
    professional mental health workers as well as conducting and directing
    group psychotherapy and meeting with community mental health agencies.

    March, 1974 - May, 1974 - 12 hours per week - Therapist for Clinton
    County Community Health Center in St. Johns, Michigan. She had duties
    in this capacity to serve as a co-therapist with former inpatients of
    the State hospital system and also to do individual psychotherapy with
    individuals with severe emotional problems.

Thus, from reviewing Ms. Becker's work experience, both full and part time, and
also her educational attainment it seems she meets the criteria for the Psychologist
10. That is, since graduating in 1973 she has acquired two years experience in
Psychology with all of her experience having been acquired after receiving the
Masters' Degree in Psychology. Her level of performance in the Reception and
Guidance Center has shown her to have a greater level of skill than would be expected at the 09 level. Her skill has been demonstrated at the level that she
has been assigned as the initial training individual for Psychologist 12 staff
members who possess doctoral degrees who are entering our system. Upon review of
all her psychological reports and her transcases they continue to demonstrate a
high level of clinical expertise.

Concerning the second part of the request you forwarded to me from Mr. Donald Tufts,
concerning the question of why the position originally was not filled at a higher
level, I can only make an educated guess as it occurred before my assuming the
duties of Administrator of the Psychological Services Unit. As you are aware we
are a maximum security penal insitution and there was considerable question on
whether or not a female psychologist could function in the setting. Ms. Becker
was the first female psychologist hired to work inside a maximum security prison
in the State. All the personnel information was sent to the S.P.S.M. Personnel
Officer. We were then informed of the level we could offer her employment. We
do not have the information on how her level was determined or who made the
determination.

JP/dmc

cc: J. Becker
     File

WARRANT NUMBER	55098435	NAME	BECKER EUGENIA W		SOCIAL SECURITY NUMBER		

	CURRENT PERIOD HOURS	EARNINGS	CODE	CURRENT PERIOD AMOUNT	YEAR-TO-DATE AMOUNT	OTHER DEDUCTIONS		NET PAY
REGULAR	80.0	532.00	FED TAX 00	78.98	78.98	LIFE INS.	.70	85.32
OVER TIME			FICA	31.12	31.12	L.T.D.	8.91	
SHIFT DIFF.			STATE TAX 00	24.47	24.47	CU10	300.00	PORTION NON TAX
SHIFT DIFF. OT			RET. 04			EA01	2.50	
			HEALTH INS.					TOTAL DEDUCTIONS
BALANCES		U.S. SAVINGS BOND DED.	GROSS	532.00	532.00			446.68
ANNUAL LEAVE	52.4		GROSS PAY ADJ.		CITY TAX			PERIOD ENDING 12 25 76
SICK LEAVE	33.0	PURCHASE	CD AMOUNT	CD EX AMOUNT				DEPARTMENT
COMP TIME								CORRECTN
TOWARD NEXT STEP	160.0	BALANCE						AGENCY
TOWARD LONGEVITY								ST PRISN
MSG A						PAY RATE	6.55	TKU 125 MAIL CODE BEC
MSG B								

See back for other deduction and city tax codes.

WARRANT NUMBER	57531491	NAME	BECKER EUGENIA W		SOCIAL SECURITY NUMBER		

PAY RATE	8.50		CODE	CURRENT PERIOD AMOUNT	YEAR-TO-DATE AMOUNT	OTHER DEDUCTIONS		NET PAY
			GROSS	680.00	6664.00	LIFE INS.	.54	188.74
	CURRENT PERIOD HOURS	EARNINGS	FICA	41.14	403.17	L.T.D.	11.56	PORTION NON-TAX
REGULAR	80.0	680.00	RET. 01			CU10	300.00	
OVER TIME			DEF. COMP			EA01	3.50	TOTAL DEDUCTIONS
SHIFT DIFF.			FED. TAX 01	103.87	1005.92			
SHIFT DIFF. OT			STATE TAX 01	28.63	280.04			491.26
GROSS PAY ADJUST			HEALTH INS.	1.81	18.10			PERIOD ENDING 04 29 78
	BALANCES		DENTAL	.21	.42			DEPARTMENT
ANNUAL LEAVE	18.9	SICK LEAVE 12.0	CITY TAX					CORRECTN
TOWARD NEXT STEP	800.0	COMP TIME						AGENCY
TOWARD LONGEVITY				U.S. SAVINGS BOND				ST PRISN
MSG A			DED.	PURCHASE	BAL			TKU 775 MAIL CODE 775
ANNUAL LEAVE ACCRUAL 4.7								

See back for other deduction and city tax codes.

thing at least, which is putting out and changing policy directives until it has your head swimming! I tried to gather up all that seemed relevant for the new people to know--- well, if not *know,* at least have on hand to look up, when necessary. My manual has now swelled to over 300 pages.

R&GC PSYCHOLOGICAL SERVICES UNIT TRAINING MANUAL FOR CLINICAL STAFF

February 1, 1977

Contents

Figure 25 - Above and following 2 pages – Table of Contents for Training Manual I compiled.

I did have to take a "time out" this spring for medical reasons, when I encountered problems with thrombosis in my leg. The doctor prescribed six weeks off work, and during that period, I became acquainted once again with the "real" world. While away from Seven Block, I began to see how working here inside the prison has actually *taken over* my life. The hours I spend each week behind the walls do not disappear from my mind, once I have punched my time card at the end of the day. Perhaps in a way, I am becoming almost as much of a member of this social order on the inside as are the residents I work with! I have begun questioning whether this is a good thing for me personally. I am also realizing how little any one person can actually accomplish that is meaningful in here, regardless of good intentions. Corrections is a closed system that swings from rehabilitation to punishment and back again, depending on shifts in leadership, and my frustration with this is growing.

However, now that I am back from medical leave, I am continuing as therapist with the same mixed group that I started with last year, and we still meet in the dreary radio room in the subhall. As I said before, Ronald came with me to a few of the sessions at first, and then let me go it alone. I feel very comfortable as the therapist of this group now, though I still question my ability to help them as much as I would like, since most of the men have such deep-seated problems.

Since I last wrote, many of the old crew I spoke of so often earlier have moved on. Some have moved up the Corrections ladder to more prestigious positions, but many others became disillusioned with the promises of change and better conditions, and found work elsewhere. New psychologists have been coming in at a rapid rate, as the exodus of others continues. We now have another female psychologist on the block--- (still no ladies room, though!) Her name is Janet and she is installed in the office beside me, as Edward is no longer working here. I don't feel I know Janet very well yet, for she tends to keep to herself. There was another woman around for a while also, a social worker, I believe, but she is no longer here and I seldom saw her anyway. What was very important to me, though, was encountering Connie for the first time. I hadn't even heard that she had been hired, and then one day as I was walking on base, there she was coming toward me. She smiled, and I knew right away that we were going to be friends. Connie is petite and pretty, and that smile seemed momentarily to bring the sunshine into Seven Block! She works under Todd Miller's direction, doing exit testing on men who will be leaving the various Jackson prison facilities, so our schedules and duties really don't overlap very often. However, we make the most of it when they do. She tells me about her little boy and her twin brother, and we talk about how working in the prison affects us. She has become a close friend here at work, and occasionally, we get together outside also. Although I do often miss the camaraderie with the Seven

October 5, 1977

1. **Question:** The three ladies employed inside 7-Block are requesting a ladies' restroom. Can this be expected in the future?

   Answer: Only problem is where. There is a possibility we could convert the mail office back to a rest area. A sliding "IN" and "OUT" sign will be pursued to be posted on existing restroom door to make it more convenient to use.

/ 2. **Question:** There have been a rash of break-ins of the Psychologists' offices. Can security be tightened up in this area?

   Answer: For the time being, Psychologists whose offices are equipped with deadbolts are rquested to use them. This will be pursued further.

3. **Question:** Approximately a year ago, there was a list drawn up and distributed among the 2-10 shift describing in detail the duties of each gallery officer. May we have another more current duty description list please? Perhaps this could benefit both the 6-2 and 2-10 shifts.

   Answer: Captain   has stated that he will pursue this and publish something in this area shortly.

4. **Question:** May we have security gates installed on the South end of Base to prevent residents from the other galleries having access to Base without authorization? This would greatly increase the physical control of the unit as now whichever end the Base Officer is on, residents come down the other end.

   Answer: This was the same problem we were having controlling the galleries, so we installed gates at either end. These, except for very rare occasions, are not used. The requisition for the fencing and gates for Base has been in for some three months and should be in soon.

5. **Question:** Would it be possible to obtain keys for both types of handcuffs we have in 7-Block. Perhaps enough keys should be obtained to equip the Desk-man, alternate Desk-man, Base Officer, and "000" officer with keys.

   Answer: Cuffs and keys are over $20 per set, and they keep disappearing. It seems some feel they must have a personal cuff key. The only time a man is cuffed in R&GC, he is taken to 5-Block. Both the Control Center and 5-Block staff have keys if we need them.

Figure 26 - Request for Ladies Room — two years after I was hired!

Block friends who have left employment here or transferred elsewhere this past year (Ronald, Paul, Don, Steve, Lou, Frank and Edward), I feel fortunate to have established such a good friendship with Connie.

Adam Rothschild became Superintendent of the Reception Center (R&GC) when Andy moved up to be Warden of SPSM. Unfortunately, the obvious animosity toward the Psychological Services Unit that Rothschild made clear when he first addressed us in the staff meeting I wrote of earlier, has not diminished. Of course, this has placed Bob and Adam Rothschild in the roles of antagonists. It is unfortunate for us all, as the psychologists in the PSU seem to be under siege, often facing hostility from the officers, from CSU, now from the Superintendent, and from Dr. Mannion, the psychiatrist who is slated to be in charge of all Mental Health Services in the prison.

Usually, though, there is nothing humorous to be said about the animosity between Superintendent Rothschild, and Bob as Administrator of PSU. But the way it came to the fore for everyone on the staff to see, one day in a staff meeting, was a bit amusing. Bob was off on medical leave, as I had convinced him that his appearance would benefit if he'd have a relatively simple operation to make his blind eye focus in coordination with the other one, though the vision, of course, would not improve. Rothschild was to conduct the staff meeting in Bob's absence, and he arrived after we had all assembled. His first statement to the group was that "Dr. Walsh cannot be with us for a while, as he is being treated for his mental problems and is hospitalized." (!) I had been sitting out of his line of vision, partly hidden by the door, and when he saw me, he did a double-take and said, "Oh hello, Jean, I didn't see you there." Obviously! Of course, I had already told the others about the procedure Bob was having done. Did I ever say that I've learned not to be surprised at anything that happens in this Unit?

Oh, on a lighter note, I can now report that at last, I have been told the full story of that green rug, which still graces the floor in my office! It wasn't until Bob and I were together that he let me know--- the rug had been purloined from his new corner office shortly after he had moved there from his old office next to mine! The former occupant of the new office was leaving employment in Corrections, and bequeathed it to Bob. Bob was delighted, as having any kind of "luxury" is very rare indeed, in Seven Block. He had been the proud owner for all of a day or two, and then arrived on Monday morning to find it gone! He immediately looked for Cowboy, who is always "in the know" about happenings in the block, but Cowboy professed ignorance, and sympathetically said, "Well, Doc, you know, it's a prison---" and he offered to get the porters to paint Bob's office floor.

It was some days later that Bob dropped into my office and saw his rug gracing my floor! He reports that his first reaction (understandably) was one of anger. But then he concluded that I was probably not involved in the heist, so he resolved to "cool it!" He didn't tell me for at least a year, and then we were able to have a good laugh about it! I believe I offered to give it back to him, but he was a gentleman and refused. Around here, it is good to have something to laugh about once in a while!

Have I mentioned before the problems those of us with offices on base encounter, when men on the galleries above us decide to make life interesting by blocking their toilets with whatever is handy? I returned from lunch one day to find that my feet were "squishing," as I walked from the door to my desk across my much-prized green rug! I have no way of knowing if this was a personal attack, or if someone up there was just bored and wanted to see what would happen! At any rate, it took a good deal of time for my rug to dry out completely, in spite of the help of the porters in the block. I am stubborn, however, and sadly, am used to unsanitary conditions by now, so the rug still graces my office floor!

I have had some interesting encounters with residents since I last wrote, also. One man that I was scheduled to interview, closed and locked the door of my office after he entered. This is not a good sign! I guess more by instinct than calculation, I refused to show alarm and firmly told him to be seated. Apparently, this reaction (or lack of one) must have deprived him of his intention of "scaring the psych," and I was able to carry on the interview without incident. Yes, I know I could have picked up the phone to call Control, but I also realize how long it would probably take custody to arrive, even if I was still able to dial the number! I hope someday, the department will realize the need to invest in some type of alarm that we can carry with us, and that will alert custody if we need their help.

Further complicating everything in the Reception Center now is the severe overcrowding. Seven Block is full and running over with new residents, to the extent that some Seven Block men are presently double-bunked in the open on the bulkheads of Eight Block, and even in one of our testing rooms. This is a situation that is both dangerous and difficult to manage. It also increases the pressure on our unit to process as many men through reception as we can, as quickly as possible.

Facing 1977

Some minor relief is expected in 1977 for Michigan's crowded prison system. The mental health facility at Ionia—Riverside Center—is to be opened in January and will eventually provide about 600 beds for male prisoners. The first of the prisoners for this facility will come from Nine Block at the Trusty Division of SPSM. Later others will come from the Reformatory. Some of the pressures associated with crowding at SPSM also should be eased this spring with the opening of the northside facility at SPSM. This medium security prison, contiguous to the main walled prison, will open intially with cell blocks 1 and 2. An additional 360 beds will be added when the funds become available. The new state law mandating an additional two years in prison for those possessing a firearm during commission of a felony is expected to add 400 prisoners to the system during 1977. The prison population on Dec. 16 was 12,409.

Figure 27 - Previous page and above — Bulkhead photo — Overcrowding!

Because I was aware of the need to somehow speed up the work we are required to do, I came forward with an idea I had been thinking about for some time. It seemed to me that a lot of the staff's time, following their interviews with new residents, is taken up with the dictation of required information that is not psychological in nature. Our dictated reports, referred to as transcases, are in narrative form and are typed by the ladies in the typing pool.

My thought was that much of the information that is necessary for classification to receive from our reports, when they are considering a man's placement, such as age, grade level, physical problems, escapes, sex offenses or a history of mental illness, and so on, could be recorded in much less time on a well-designed, thorough, checklist-type form. And actually, it occurred to me that many of our psychological recommendations could also be made through such a form. That would leave only the psychologist's Clinical Opinions section that would need to be dictated. I was given the go-ahead to design such a form, and the final version was given an OK from Lansing and was put into use this year! I also trained our PSU staff on its use, and received a "job well done" from the Director himself!

STATE OF MICHIGAN

DEPARTMENT OF CORRECTIONS

RECEPTION AND GUIDANCE CENTER RECOMMENDATION

NAME	NUMBER	AGE	STA-TUS	READING: MATH:	A.G.E.	TERMS	PLACE-MENT	DATE
		17	C	R-3.3 M-4.8		7½-15 2-4	I	4-6-77

RECOMMENDATION: CLOSE	TRANSFERRED

MANAGEMENT: IONIA CLOSE is seemingly required by Mr. _____ who is in need of psychological or psychiatric health and who had a sex offense on his record at a very early age. This interviewer has referred Mr. _____ to the Clinical Services Unit, as test results and Mr. _____ behavior during the interview suggests his need for contact with psychological staff. Mr. _____ has no pending charges and no escapes on his record. STATISTICAL RISK POTENTIAL: HIGH VIOLENCE RISK as Mr. _____ is single and is incarcerated for an assaultive offense. He was apparently raised by his grandmother.

EDUCATION: REMEDIAL CLASSES are required for Mr. _____ because of very deficient scores in reading and math. However, it seems likely that underlying psychopathology is interfering with Mr. _____ abilities to cope with a testing situation. He progressed through the ninth grade in the community. Although he tested to be functioning in the borderline defective range intellectually, this interviewer feels that this is a somewhat low estimate of his potential.

JOB READINESS: A ROUTINE WORK ASSIGNMENT is initially sufficient for Mr. _____ until such time as his academic scores and emotional stability are such that he may be placed in a trade training program. Mr. _____ was 16 years of age when incarcerated for the instant offense, and has virtually no work experience in the community. He specified an interest in auto mechanics, computer programming, and custodial functions.

SUBSTANCE ABUSE: NO RECOMMENDATION is made for Mr. _____ who does not appear to have either a drug or alcohol problem.

PHYSICAL HEALTH: NO RECOMMENDATION is made for Mr. _____ in the absence of a medical clearance in his file.

TRANSFER AS INDICATED ABOVE IS HEREBY ORDERED

DIRECTOR OF CLASSIFICATION	DATE	DEPUTY DIRECTOR IN CHARGE OF BUREAU OF CORRECTIONAL FACILITIES

DMS/dmw

STATUS: F-FIRST TERM. C- FIRST TERM-CONC. SENT. R-REPEATER. N-PVNS, V-TECH. VIOL.. E-ESCAPE SENT.. L-LIFERS-LONG SENT.. M- MURDER 1ST

PLACEMENT: J-SPSM, W- CAMPS. M- MARQUETTE. I- REFORMATORY. T-TRAINING UNIT C- CASSIDY LAKE.D-DHC, K-MUSKEGON Q- MIPC

CRO- 101

R&GC – RECOMMENDATION

Figure 28 - Above and following page – Transcases were dictated by the psychologist prior to my idea of simplifying the process with a checklist with five carbon copies.

CLINICAL IMPRESSIONS: During the interview, communication was quite difficult with Mr. _____ who appeared on numerous occasions to be about to divulge deeply distressing feelings, but whose apparent lack of trust interfered. At one point, when questioned about a previous sex offense, he began to cry. He also refused to speak of this offense and blamed the interviewer for mentioning it and upsetting him. Mr. _____ was able to verbalize his fears that he needs help, by that meaning for his mental health. It was difficult to understand his verbalizations, as he turned his head away from the interviewer and often kept his fingers in his mouth. This appears to be a very disturbed young man, and due to the communication difficulties and time pressures, this interviewer referred him to the Clinical Services Unit for an evaluation. The instant offense seems quite bizarre and Mr. _____ himself has no explaination for his actions in which he threatened to kill an old man. Apparently, he recalls going out of control when verbally abused by this individual but he has little explaination as to the intensity of his reaction, which he realizes could have resulted in the death of this man as well as the policeman who apprehended him. He also has no satisfactory reason for being so heavily armed, but does, with difficulty, confide his fears of other individuals. Mr. _____'s psycholofical tests show regression and possible indications of underlying schizophrenia. His DAP is quite primitive and shows both hostility and a poor self-image. Mr. _____ no doubts suffers from the realization of his mother's total rejection of him, and his father's absence. He was raised by his grandmother because of his alcoholic mother's neglect. It is difficult to see a more productive future for Mr. _____ unless he can attain intensive help through the therapy program.

TREATMENT OBJECTIVES: INDIVIDUAL PSYCHOTHERAPY is initially recommended for Mr. _____ with the aim being to bring him to the point of acceptance of group psychotherapy. At present, his suspicion and lack of trust are such that he would probably refuse group psychotherapy. If he can make gains through individual contacts, group psychotherapy for sex offenders appears the most relevant program. Mr. _____ was unable to relate the circumstances of the attempted rape on his record, but this was obviously very distressing to him.

Jean Becker, Clinical Psychologist

4-4-77
JB/add
4-5-77

Orig: _____
  cc: Counselor
      Lansing Record Office (2)
      Institutional Main File
      Psych File

159

BASIC INFORMATION

PLACEMENT   RECOMMENDED BY

☐ MAX ☐ CLOSE ☐ MED ☐ MIN
☐ SEGR - ADMIN/PROTECTION

By Authority PD-BCF 34.01   By Authority MCL 791.264

TRANSFER AS INDICATED ABOVE IS HEREBY ORDERED

0 2 0 5 3 8	BIRTHDATE	4 0	AGE
U S	CITIZENSHIP	0 0	DEPENDENTS
0 3 0 3 7 8	DATE OF INTERVIEW

CLASSIFICATION COMMITTEE:

MANAGEMENT

CRITERIA:

X Pending Charge/Hold/Probation Violation

PD

SOURCE CODES
I: Interview
T: Tests
P: PSI
IR: Institutional Record
CR: Community Record

| Offense | Max. Time | Docket No. | Jurisdiction | I | T | P | IR | CR |

X History of ☐ Arson ☐ Drug Sales ☒ Assault ☒ Sex Offenses

X Medical-Psychological Considerations ☐ None
Physical Problem   Complaint ____
Special Diet/Medication (type) ____
Severe Psychological Problem/Hospitalization X Past ____ Present
Suicide Potential/Chronic Depression ____ Past ____ Present

____ Escape History ☒ None
☐ Adult Institution ____ Close ____ Medium ____ Minimum Within ☐ Years
☐ Juvenile Institution Within ☐ Years
☐ AWOL Within ☐ Years
☐ Other (specify) ____ Within ☐ Years

X Policy Psych Case [X] [P] [X] [CR] ____ Adjustment Problems ☐ None
____ Mental Hospital Within 2 Years ____ Guilty but Mentally III
X Predatory Sexual Offenses X Violent Crime with Injury or Death
____ Institutional Assaults X Assaultive Pattern
X Sadism/Torture/Physical Cruelty ____ Belligerent to Authority
Screening Date ____/____/____ ____ Homosexual Tendencies ____ Predatory ____ Passive
____ Co-Defendent/Enemy in System: ____ Poor Prior Adjustment
    X Deficient Coping Skills

| Name | Number | Place | Name | Number | Place |

STATISTICAL VIOLENCE RISK

PREDICTION: ____ Very High X High ____ Middle ____ Low ____ Very Low ____ Insuf. Data

CRITERIA:

[0 1] Number of Prior Prison Terms [0 2] Number of Adult Probations
____ Juvenile Record ☐ Before Age 15 ☐ Commitment ☐ Probation ☐ Age at 1st Arrest
☒ Married at Offense or Prior ☐ Current ☐ Never
____ Raised by Mother X Instant Offense Assaultive

| I | T | P | IR | CR |

PAROLE CONTRACT

____ Accepted X Not Eligible ____ Declined by Client Objectives:

COMMENTS: SEE PSYCH REPORT

**RECEPTION & GUIDANCE CENTER
RECOMMENDATIONS**

Figure 29 - Above and following 2 pages – A sample of the Transcase Form I designed to replace the one that was dictated. Only the Clinician's Opinions are dictated. Note that the Clinician no longer makes a recommendation for placement due to the many variables confronting the Classification Committee. Their decision is entered last, in Basic Information at top of page one.

160

EDUCATIONAL PREPAREDNESS

RECOMMENDATION __X__ Remedial ____ High School ____ G.E.D. ____ College ____ None

CRITERIA:

Reading Level `05`   Math Level `03`   Date Tested **2-26-78**

Lacks high school diploma or G.E.D.

`06` Prior academic achievement (specify) _____

Unmotivated/dropped out of school (expelled)

Limiting physical disability (specify) _____

Intellectual factors (specify) _____

Motivated for academic achievement _____

	I	T	P	IR	CR
			X		
	■				X
			X		

Comments: POOR MOTIVATION

JOB READINESS

RECOMMENDATION ____ Trade Training _X_ Routine Work _X_ O.J.T. ____ Voc. Counseling ____ None

Suggested Areas _____
Primary _____ Secondary

CRITERIA:

	I	T	P	IR	CR
Unstable work record/poor work habits			X		
Limited skill attainment/no marketable skills/no vocational identity		■	X		
Failed to apply skills from previous training/non-use present skills			X		
☐ Occupational identity/experience (specify) NONE	X	■	X		
Limiting disability (specify)					
Motivated for application of training NO	X		X		
Insufficient time					
Lacks entry level skills for training	■				

GATB STRENGTH: G V N S P Q K F M   OAP'S _____
Primary _____ Secondary

Comments: GATB INVALID

SUBSTANCE ABUSE

RECOMMENDATION ☐ Drug Program   ☒ Alcohol Program   ☐ None

CRITERIA:

			I	T	P	IR	CR
Alcohol	☒ Habitual Excessive Use/Addicted	☐ Episodic Excessive Use		■	X		
Opiates	☐ Habitual Excessive Use/Addicted	☐ Episodic Excessive Use					
Other ____ (Specify)	☐ Habitual Excessive Use/Addicted	☐ Episodic Excessive Use					
	____ Denies Problem						

Comments: _____

THERAPEUTIC PROGRAMMING

RECOMMENDATION ____ Individual Counseling _X_ Group Counseling ☐ None
____ Individual Psychotherapy ____ Group Psychotherapy

TYPE OF PSYCHOTHERAPY GROUP

____ Drug Dependent _X_ Sex Offender ____ Health Care Follow-up
_X_ Alcohol Dependent ____ Impulse Control ____ General

TREATMENT GOALS: BETTER IMPULSE CONTROL, ANGER MANAGEMENT

DISTRIBUTION: White - Institution; Green - Counselor; Canary - Lansing
Pink - P.S.U.; Golden Rod - Data Systems

CLINICIAN _____

CSO-104A 8/77 Page 2

CLINICIAN'S OPINIONS

Mr. _____'s underlying hostility toward women, aggravated by his own feelings of sexual inadequacy, have been underlying factors in his behavior in the past, but without the severity of the instant offense. The file reports accusations that he was responsible for obscene phone calls, and after his last incarceration, was returned as a Parole Violator for forcing a woman's car off the road. What would have followed is unknown, as a passerby intervened. However, it does seem apparent that Mr. _____ has the capability of acting out sexually, particularly when he has been drinking. His two marriages have failed, and present reports are that he was at times physically abusive, and that his second wife is very much in fear of him. It is certainly to be hoped that Mr. _____ will gain some insights into his underlying feelings prior to his release. Presently, he is blaming all of his antisocial and aggressive behaviors on the fact that he is an alcoholic. He has no understanding of why he drinks, or that he probably uses alcohol both as an escape from his own feelings of inadequacy, and as an excuse which allows him to avoid guilt feelings for violent behaviors. Mr. _____ seems to have lived up to his label of "black sheep" of his family and current psychological tests do indicate his difficulties in relating closely with other people as well as antisocial tendencies and the likelihood of his overreacting in stressful situations. Mr. _____ is particularly apt to act out when his adequacy as a male is threatened. He would be most likely to act out on individuals he perceives as weaker than himself. In the past, participation in sports have allowed him some opportunity to vent his aggressive feelings relatively harmlessly. A psychological evaluation in the past described Mr. _____ as immature, aggressive, inadequate, poorly motivated, and with a poor prognosis. All of these descriptions appear very timely even after the passage of so many years. Again, Group Therapy may prove helpful, although Mr. _____ will very likely have a great deal of difficulty facing up to the responsibility for his own actions. Without some change through therapeutic programming, this interviewer feels that Mr. _____ does constitute a threat to the safety of other individuals, particularly women and those weaker than himself.

                                        Jean Becker
                                        Clinical Psychologist

3-2-78
JB/vj
3-3-78

CLINICIAN _____Jean Becker_____

Strangely, Superintendent Rothschild's dislike of Bob does not seem to have spilled over onto me to any extent, and he has appointed me to carry out a number of special projects. Recently, he asked me to be the representative of the Reception Center to work with Lansing Office on the implementation of a new computer system! This came about because when I was with Social Services a few years ago, I worked in the computer unit as a research analyst--- though most of my work there had little to do with computers!

Rothschild also assigned me to work with Todd Miller on a thorough analysis of the entire processing system in the Reception Center. Todd and I work well together. This analysis of the movement of men through R&GC, and the subsequent planning, with Todd, of three potential alternatives, took up a great deal of my work time this past summer.

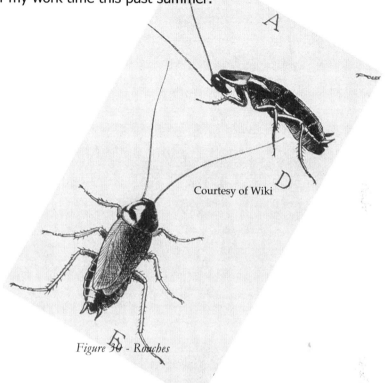

Courtesy of Wiki

Figure 30 - Roaches

And speaking of conditions---the roach problem continues. Bob encountered one that is several inches in length, and encased it in clear plastic for use as a paperweight! One actually crawled up my boot and onto my leg under my slacks! At that, I did call for the exterminator to come and spray my office, but I soon found that the smell of the chemicals they use (which is overpowering at first) remains for days, due to the lack of ventilation in my small, windowless office.

The food in the OD, well, I will be generous and say that I can see no improvement. In fact, I almost gave up eating there at all, for a while. You see, one noon as I was drinking milk through a straw, I suddenly found that the straw was blocked, and when I removed it from the glass--- well, you may be able to guess. There was a dead cockroach at the end of my straw!!

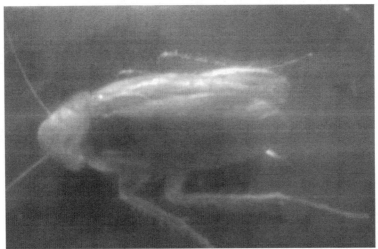

Photos by Judy Gail Krasnow

Figure 31 - Bob's roach encased in clear plastic for use as a paperweight. The roach is 3.5 inches diagonally from tip of antenna to tip of rear leg. These enlarged photos don't exaggerate very much.

TO: Wardens Foltz, Egeler and Koehler, DATE: January 21, 1977
    Superintendents Abshire, Anderson, Buchko,
    Bergman, Handlon, Wheeler, Wells and Wittebols

FROM: Jack A. Boehm, Administrator *Jack A. Boehm*

SUBJECT: INSTITUTION CMIS COORDINATOR

As outlined at the Wardens and Superintendents meeting, the Department
has approval to purchase a five mini-computer system to support CMIS.
In an effort to get the equipment and system installed, we will need
a close working relationship with the department's various functional
areas and in particular, those locations where equipment or terminals
are to be installed.

We are asking that you appoint a liaison person to work with the CMIS
Planning and Development Unit analysts. This person should be in a
position to speak for you and to negotiate and resolve differences that
may arise in your functional area. Also, this person will need to be able
to coordinate the various activities that will be required to the area
of site preparation; space readiness, power, conditioning, security, etc.

As soon as all liaison people are identified there will be a meeting at
which time we will go over the plans, schedule and specific needs of the
system. This meeting will include the systems analysts that are developing and installing the system who will be assigned to a specific institution as contact person.

We would like to have your liaison person identified by February 1, 1977.
If you have questions on making a selection, please do not hesitate to
call. Funds for payment of travel expenses to this liaison meeting are
provided in our L.E.A.A. grant. Please let me know if you need travel
funds for the meeting.

TO: C. E. Anderson, Superintendent DATE: February 1, 1977
    Reception and Guidance Center

FROM: , Ph.D.
    Administrator, Psychological Services Unit
SUBJECT:

The representative from our unit who has been nominated to represent the Reception
and Guidance Center in the CMIS Meeting is Ms. Eugenia Becker. She has been nominated
for the CMIS Committee because of her background in dealing with computerized pro-
graming with the Michigan Department of Social Services. She will work closely
with Mr.   , Captain   and Lt.   in discussing the security aspects of
the computer terminals in the Reception and Guidance Center.

JP/dmc

cc: J. Becker
    Lt.
    Capt.

    File

*Figure 32 - I am appointed liaison person to represent R&GC concerning implementation of the new
statewide computer system.*

165

TO: Deputy Director Brown   DATE: 8/2/77

IS FROM: Warden Anderson

SUBJECT: Intake Analysis - Reception and Guidance Center

Attached you will find copy of a very excellent report put together
by   and Jean Becker, Reception and Guidance Center.

I have discussed the report with Dr.   as well as   and
Jean. After going over all of the items, I feel their recommendations
should be implemented in the Reception and Guidance Center and have
instructed staff to proceed accordingly.

CEA:ao

cc: Dr.

     Jean Becker

     P.S.   - Proceed to implement the recommendations.

TO: Warden Anderson   DATE: 9-14-77

ENT

ONS FROM: Robert Brown, Jr.

SUBJECT: Intake Analysis - Reception and Guidance Center

On 8-2-77, you forwarded to me a copy of the Analysis of Intake Process
completed by   and Jean Becker. Their report was dated July 21,
1977. Both   and Jean should be commended for their effort and what
appears to be excellent work. I concur with your instructions to the staff to
proceed accordingly. As recommendations are implemented, care should be
taken to clearly think through what affect the change will have on other
agencies, both within our Department and outside the Department.

RB:evb

Figure 33 - The Testing Director and I are to conduct a systems analysis and make recommendations.
They were approved by the deputy director and implemented.

In spite of some improvement, the ongoing exodus of discontented staff continues. The conditions in Seven Block for those of us who work here have not improved significantly. A representative from Lansing met with us at a staff meeting, where we expressed our anger over the disparity in our pay compared with that of other, less highly trained employees. No action was taken. Is this an indication of how little they value the work we do??

I was also the unlucky psychologist scheduled to interview the Detroit rapist, appropriately known as "Bigfoot." As I perused the file, which described some eleven rapes, I was not at all sure I wanted to start my day this way! I did call Edward, who still occupied the office next door at that time, and asked that he plan to be there for the next half hour and to be alert for anything unusual he might hear through the wall! However, when I called the large man into my office, he shuffled in and slumped down into the chair, and I had the immediate feeling that he was afraid of *me!* He was far from forthcoming in the interview, but the files and my own impressions were sufficient for my report.

Just when I felt that nothing would ever shock me again, the door opened and a young man entered and sat down. He had his possessions clutched in his arms. And then I saw his hands--- or rather the bandaged stumps where his hands had been! I tried to talk with him, though his anger and hostility became obvious right away. I did learn that his cell had been torched by other inmates, while he was in detention at Ionia. Apparently he had been treated there initially, and then was returned to SPSM. Beyond that, I could get nothing from him, not even what he wanted me to do for him. I ordered him to come with me, and we walked up to Control together. I told the officers that I did not want the man locked in general population and that he should be taken to the hospital immediately. Then I went back to my office and tried to calm down. I have been terribly afraid of fires ever since I saw my grandparents badly burned after their house exploded when I was eleven, so dealing with this was especially difficult for me.

I have finally had another experience I will never forget, that of being present in Seven Block when a shot was fired, apparently to break up an altercation that threatened to get out of hand. It is hard to describe the intensity of the sound and the reverberations. The sudden, intense fear that this could turn into something ugly and threatening was there for me, as well. I found myself sending up a brief prayer--- but I imagine the shock of the shot, rather than my prayer, was what ended the event!

Later

October 7th, 1977

I had a premonition that this was going to be a bad day, probably because I dread the trek needed to get me over to group therapy on Wednesdays. And to top it all off, it had to be raining buckets on the way to work. We (Bob and I) ran from the parking lot to the main building to punch in, passing through the middle of the surly group of hall porters, as they listened to hard rock music in their small space with benches, just inside the door. We punched in around 7:55, and then went to consult today's menu, which was taped up on the window of the store. Oh dear, Polish sausage--- a particularly bad noon meal in the OD. Well, then it was time for the dash through the rain to the bubble--- a run of about 300 or more feet. I envy the *men* who work on Seven Block, because they can cut through Six Block to avoid getting wet, but I'm not allowed to do that anymore. I have to go outside after punching in, and go the long way around to get to the bubble. That's true in reverse, too, every time I want to leave Seven Block to go somewhere else in the prison.

Once we're at the bubble, I confer with Bob in Rothschild's office. (I liked it better when it was Andy's!) We talk about the best way to get one of my group men a compassionate furlough so he can be with his wife, who's to undergo brain surgery. Bob wants to know if I can vouch for him, psychologically, if they allow him to go without a guard. I hesitate. I like Bernard, but he did rape someone--- But I agree. I know I am being paid to make decisions like that. I pick up a lot of papers, which are work left over from yesterday, and I sigh--- there is so little time. Connie offers me a ride back to the main building, as she's on her way to Trusty today. She agrees to delay a few minutes when I ask her to, because I'd prefer not to be early, as it's a lonely walk down the subhall to group in the radio room. There are usually dozens, maybe as many as 50 inmates there, eyeing me as I pass the crosswalk and go beyond into the subhall. When I'm on time, my group men are there waiting, sometimes still in the hall, and I'm pretty sure they'd help me if there was trouble.

So I finally ride over from the bubble with Connie, she lets me off, and I go back through the hallway with the porters sitting on their benches, but I'm alone this time. Cutting through this way is a shorter route to SPSM proper than through the main entrance, but if it wasn't raining, I might have gone around to that door instead. Only one of the porters speaks, and with exaggerated politeness. The porters used to be a nice group. Now they are new and hostile, a sea of black faces. I don't like being alone there, so I move quickly. I stop in GOS to pick up a file, then go to the main gate and wait for it to grind open. It does, and I walk quickly through the metal detector and past the gate operator behind the bullet-proof glass. Then I have to wait for the second gate to open. I speak to the officer. No answer.

As I go through the Rotunda, I see Bernard and the others in my group who have to come over from Trusty, as they are about to enter the room where the guard will do a strip search. No wonder they sometimes question whether group therapy is worth all the indignity! Bernard quickly passes me a letter he wants me to read--- it's from his ex-wife. I stand on the steps of the rotunda reading it. She's threatening to kill his present wife. Ironic, as the lady is probably dying anyway.

Then I continue on alone, as my men are entering the rotunda to go to the control desk. I cross the huge area, then go by myself into the subhall with offices on each side. It isn't too bad here, before you get to the crosswalk--- quite a few civilian personnel, as well as residents, have business here. The officer at the gate at the far end by the crosswalk recognizes me, and nods as I thank him for opening the gate for me. I hurriedly cross the open hallway connecting the north and south yards, trying not to collide with the crowds of residents. I push open the gate to the restricted end of the subhall. "Only Authorized Personnel." There are many men milling around, inside today because of the rain. There are no other staff or guards in sight. I hurry. Down at the end of the hall, I see Rubin, one of my group members, waiting. His is one familiar face out of a sea of hostile ones. Rubin is cadre in Seven Block, and has been trying to convince me to take him on in individual psychotherapy in my office in the block. I think I probably will, when I can find the time. Cadre have been reassuringly protective of me ever since I began work here.

Although the composition of this therapy group has changed some from a year ago, a number of the men I started with are still here. The group is a mixture, consisting of a few sex offenders along with those who have committed assaultive type crimes. Sex offenders in a mixed group often refuse to acknowledge that there is a sexual component to their crimes, as this might make them a target for the dislike and even hatred many inmates have for sex offenders. Pedophiles, in particular, are fearful of being known for their predatory actions toward children. I did have several members of this group whose files mentioned sex offenses.

One of these men, though, was serving a sentence this time for another assaultive offense. As could have been predicted, he never brought up the earlier sex offense with a child, and I felt I should not force him to confront this in a mixed group. The man came into the group at the start depressed and hostile, and for some time refused to participate at all. Then he (Joe) did begin to open up, about what it is like being a Vietnam veteran, his disillusionment upon returning home, and how his anger had entered into the crimes he had committed. I had felt that he was beginning some real work on his problems at last, when I found that he was up for parole. I had been thankful that I did not have to do a parole evaluation on him, (we are no longer required to do them on our group men, though we can confer with the psychologist who is assigned the job) because I was uneasy, knowing he had not yet fully confronted his deep-seated anger, *or* his earlier sex offense. However, when a parole board member called my office and suddenly asked me outright if Joe hadn't worked hard and now deserved another chance, I was unprepared, caught my breath, and mumbled something of an assent. If I was wrong, I haven't done either Joe or society any favor. I wonder if the parole board will ever realize that attending group therapy for a certain number of months is no guarantee of a man's future behavior! Those of us who are therapists know that, although it seems worthwhile for us to keep trying, because somehow, we do manage to help a few.

Another member of the group, Greg, had several sex offenses in his file, and again, we did not deal with this in group. Greg, however, has been using his lengthy sentence to take college courses, mostly in psychology! Immediately in the group sessions, he put himself in the position of something of a wannabe co-therapist. I will admit, he was skillful in getting other group members to open up. I will also admit that I was not experienced enough then to know how to handle the situation very well. So as long as he wasn't overstepping too much, I let his "helping" continue, since the others didn't seem to resent it. But one day not long ago, Greg announced in group that he was up for parole also, and that he *expected* me to do his parole evaluation! I told him that I could not do that, that it was not even an issue now, as we are no longer allowed to evaluate our group members--- and right there in group, Greg exploded! He had suddenly found that his skillful maneuvering into a favorable position with the therapist had all been to no avail, and his anger and language knew no bounds! Fortunately, he must have realized that any physical attack on me would probably be thwarted by other group members, and would most certainly result in an additional charge of assault. I will admit, though, that when he slammed the radio room door as he left, I was hoping I would never have to see him again. And so far I haven't, though I did give considerable input to the staff member who was assigned to do his evaluation!

Many of the group members, however, seem to have benefitted from the interactions in the group. Whether the gains will last once they confront situations in the "real" world again, will remain to be seen. One of the men who has worked very hard in group is Benny, the transvestite who suddenly tends to lose control when he sees an attractive woman, and assaults her. This is something I am trying to make some sense of, not just for his sake, but also because he has a wife and children who love him. Benny is very personable, and has been willing to talk in the group about his rage impulses, and his fetish of wearing women's clothing in private since childhood. I would like to think that his real efforts in group will lead to some breakthrough, but I will admit that my hopes for him are just that--- hopes.

Then there is Chet, who killed a man while on drugs, and who received a life sentence when he was only nineteen. He is in his twenties, now, and knowing him at present, it is hard to believe the story of his violent action. He seems to have transformed himself while in prison, and has done all that he can to take advantage of prison offerings, such as college courses, and becoming part of the group who help with the braille program. His insights in group therapy appear to be genuine, and he is helpful to the others. He writes me lengthy letters once in a while that are pleasant and informative, not demanding, and he recently enclosed a letter he had received from his father. That letter touched me, for it helped me see that Chet's family continues to love him very much in spite of his mistakes, which surely must have hurt them deeply. In the letter, his dad includes details of all the things that are happening in the family group, as though they fully anticipate that Chet will someday be there with them once again. How I do hope that through some miracle, that may happen.

Another group member who recently paroled is a man named John. He was a first offender for an armed robbery. In our sessions, he spoke sometimes, but was usually quiet, though he always seemed interested in what was taking place. I can't say that I felt I really got to know him. However, after he paroled, I received a letter from him in which he vowed he would never let me down by committing another offense. And he also said that although we would never see each other again, he wanted me to understand the depth of his feeling for me, and also how much my willingness to be there to try and help, had meant to him. Again, I felt humbled and was touched.

The young man who entered therapy while on crutches, Reggie, is something of a conundrum. He steadfastly denies he is guilty, and blames the offense on his twin brother who, he maintains, let him go to prison for something he didn't do. When questioned about the leg, it was clear that he didn't want to talk about it. Because of his appearance (he is slender and ties his blond hair in back), I suspected predators may have had a great deal to do with his injuries. However, I wasn't sure what I could do about the situation, as long as he was unwilling to trust me enough to talk with me, either directly, or in the group. He seemed depressed and angry at the world, but continued to attend our group sessions. A solution came from an unexpected direction, however. One day as I was walking in the subhall toward the OD, I saw a small group of residents coming toward me, and one of them, who seemed to be the leader, broke away from the others, addressed me by name and asked if he could speak with me. I nodded. He said he needed my help getting Reggie locked somewhere safe, because "I don't want to have to hurt the kid anymore." He went on to say that he had put in for a transfer to Marquette Prison, and that after that happens, Reggie will be all right. Was this a sexual predator with a conscience?? What a strange encounter! But at least it gave me an indication of what I must do. To make a long story short, I managed to have Reggie locked in the protection of Six Block temporarily, and after the danger was over, he resumed coming to group and is still with us. He even manages to say a few words, now and then, but still insists he is innocent. A look at his file, though, makes his story seem very doubtful.

Later

I think I will try to continue writing, but due to time pressure, I will only be commenting from time to time on things that happen, or that I am thinking about and want to be able to remember some day in the future! I know that our memories are often unreliable after time passes, and this is a part of my life that should be recorded at the time. It is hard for me to believe that I have been working at SPSM for nearly two years. But I am feeling more and more that my time here is limited, as my frustration with conditions keeps growing. Also, I know that I still do become more emotionally involved than I should in situations that arise, but that I am unable to control. It is really helpful that Bob and I are living together now, for he is able to understand my feelings. I had experienced before how impossible it is to explain to someone not familiar with the prison, why it is so difficult for me to let go of the day's happenings when the gates slam shut behind me. But now, I will go on writing about some of the events I want to recall in the future--- as well as about some I would really like to forget!

There has been some heartbreaking news. Connie has cancer. She has left work at the prison and is receiving treatment, but apparently the prognosis is not very good. She has moved to Lansing and is staying with family there. I feel loss, but also an unfocused anger, because among all the injustices that are rampant in a place like this, this one seems more meaningless and undeserved. I know, I know. Life goes on. But one little bright spot that appeared briefly in this dark and forbidding place, is now gone.

On a lighter note, very early this year, I remember one morning being asked on the phone to come up to the Control desk in Seven Block and talk with a man the officer *said* they were having difficulty controlling. When I arrived, before they brought the man in, they told me that he kept refusing to keep his clothes on, and would I please talk with him about it. I wasn't sure if this was a real problem or if they were having fun with me, especially when the resident they couldn't control turned out to be a dwarf, and he was fully clothed at the time! I did decide to talk with Mr. Engleberg, in the presence of several officers, and he didn't refute what they were saying about his behavior. He kept staring at me while nodding in agreement with what I was asking of him. As I was gathering up my things, ready to leave, the small man slid off his chair. He walked over in front of me, looked up at me and very seriously stated, "I *wuv* you."

Something remarkably positive for me happened earlier this year. I was on my way to my therapy group and was hurrying down the subhall. It was fairly crowded with residents, as usual. One man walking alone suddenly came toward me, and I immediately recognized him as the man in Six Block who had seemed so apprehensive when I first began passing his cell on my way to the OD. He smiled, and began pulling something out from under the front of his shirt, saying, "I made this for you--- I know you'll understand." And he was rapidly gone from view up the subhall, as I stood there, the recipient of a small, wrapped package. I slid it into the folders I was carrying, and unwrapped it as soon as I was alone and had an opportunity. It was a piece of wood, nicely finished, and painstakingly carved on both front and back with unworldly faces and figures, the contents of the daily nightmare of fear that had been endured by this man. However, the face carved in the very center was smiling.

Indeed I do believe I understand what he was showing me! I also understood that he had been able to come out of that lonely cell in the protection unit and was now mingling in general population. And yes, I would like to think that he was also telling me that my simple act of smiling and speaking to him, had made a difference in his life. I haven't seen the man again and I don't even know his name, but I know I will never forget him. It was as though he was showing me that my working in the prison might have had an impact for good that I am not normally aware of, in the midst of so much discouragement. Although I know full well that it is against the prison rules for staff to accept gifts from inmates, I am breaking the rules, for I will never part with this particular gift that holds so much meaning for both the giver and the recipient.

Figure 34 - Wood carving

A few of the officers in Seven Block, including one I will call Jones, especially seem to get enjoyment out of making life more difficult for me. It is usually harmless joking, though, or episodes like the interview with the dwarf. However, one day I felt that Officer Jones carried it just a bit too far. I had been buzzed into the ramp, as usual when I arrived at work, and as usual, had to wait for Jones to unlock the door at the Seven Block end. While I was waiting, control in the bubble buzzed the door there open again, and about ten new inmates in their blues marched into the ramp. Then suddenly, both doors were locked, with me inside with all the new men. I caught a glimpse of Jones grinning through the glass, but he kept us waiting for several minutes before he unlocked the Seven Block door. I remained outwardly calm throughout, but came close to losing it when Jones grabbed me and put his arms around me as I entered the block. He said, "Don't I get a little reward for letting you in??" I did a pirouette out of his grasp, laughed, and said, "Oh Jones, behave yourself!" I continued on to my office, but I will admit, I was so angry I could have committed an assault, then and there! I didn't because all of us on the PSU staff know quite well that our safety, even our lives, might sometime depend on quick action from the officers stationed on Seven Block.

I have had several other therapy groups this past year, as well as continuing the first one that I described earlier. I was co-therapist with Edward for a time, and regret to say that we did not work well together, and parted not on the best of terms, when he left employment at PSU. I think I mentioned earlier that Edward was quite open about disliking inmates, and in the group it became obvious. I felt that his attitude was detrimental to the forming of trust within the group. The last straw for me, though, was when he wrote a termination report on one of our group men that was almost entirely negative, when I thought the man had been trying hard in the group. Worse yet, he did not even inform me that he was writing the report, nor did he provide me with a copy or ask for my signature as co-therapist. This was not protocol, and I countered his report as best I could by composing one that contained my more affirmative view of the man's progress.

I was also co-therapist with Dr. Marvin Albert, who was promoted into Bob's (earlier Ronald's) old position in PSU, after Bob became Administrator. The group we led together was a sex offender group held out in Trusty Division. Both of us were able to develop some rapport with most of the group members, although one man who had committed violent rapes made me feel apprehensive throughout our sessions. Sometimes I would arrive before Marvin, and a few times I conducted the group by myself when Marvin was elsewhere. One such time, the man I referred to was participating and was talking directly to me, but he was wearing one of those styles of sunglasses that are mirrors as you look at the person. I became exasperated by not being able to see his eyes, and without thinking, I suddenly demanded sharply that he "Take those things off!" It was a tense moment, but he slowly reached up and removed the glasses. Thank goodness!

One man in the group, Daniel, had committed a rape, in large part because he had a physical problem (now corrected) and had felt he would be unable to have a normal physical relationship because of it. Clearly, he was still very shy around women. One day I arrived at group by myself, for Marvin hadn't yet arrived. I was surprised when Daniel met me at the door, asked me if he could take my coat, helped me with it, and then indicated the chair that had been saved for me. All of the other men were grinning, and it became apparent that they had taken it upon themselves to teach Daniel the proper way to treat a lady! Eventually, Daniel was paroled, and some time later, Marvin and I received an invitation to his wedding! This seems to be one happy ending, at least!

Tony— Whatever things were wrong in your life before, the Tony I know is a warm, likeable person. You've developed a lot of understanding of yourself and others, and it seems as though you're about ready to reach out even more to others and discover how great that is. I'll miss the silent communication we had going in group, and I hope you'll make a good life for yourself on the outside.

Figure 35 - I wrote notes to my group men before leaving my employment with Department of Corrections.

1978

Staff members come and go at a rapid rate, and Bob does his best, but has considerable difficulty enticing good clinicians to even *consider* working here! I didn't have a chance to write about some of the psychs I trained, who have already left for something better. Some of the new people who remain working here presently have become friends. But I must say that there are a few of my colleagues who are more difficult to categorize! I think that Karl would be one of those, because of a recent incident. Karl had volunteered to work on a committee with Todd Miller and me, to do some more work for Adam Rothschild. We had set up a meeting in Todd's office when all three of us felt we had a bit of space on our busy calendars. When the time came, Todd and I were there, but there was no sign of Karl. After quite a wait, we tried calling his office, and no one answered. Finally, with the afternoon frittering away, Todd and I decided to get to work without Karl. After we had accomplished quite a bit, I left to return to my office and was walking on base when I encountered Karl, finally on his way to Todd's office. I informed him that we hadn't known where he was, so had finished the meeting that day without him. Well, my message evidently pushed the wrong buttons on Karl! He became furious, and right there in the block full of inmates, shouted out that I was a bitch, along with a few other expletives!! I guess by now I wouldn't have been surprised to get such a message from a resident--- but from another psychologist?? I was upset, and called Bob, who ordered Karl into his office and I guess, "read him the riot act." I wasn't present, but according to Bob, Karl then appealed to Superintendent Rothschild, who came into the block and settled the matter by informing Karl that he had been entirely out of line!

Another of the new employees was a man named Sam--- and I will withhold his last name. During training, he seemed very personable and I found him to be reasonably well trained and willing to learn the Seven Block ropes. Then, after only a few weeks, there began to be rumors of some inappropriate behavior on his part with some of the ladies in the typing pool. Shortly after that, as I was driving home from work, I noticed his car behind me. He followed me all the way home! About that same time, a deputy who was bringing new men to the bubble spotted Sam, and was shocked when told he was employed as a psychologist here. He reported to Rothschild that Sam had committed sex offenses with women prisoners while working in the county jail! Bob and Marvin began an investigation, and found that although his education and previous work history did qualify him for work in the PSU, what Sam had omitted in his application was his record as a sex offender! However, he had not been prosecuted for his actions, apparently, just fired from his job. And that has happened to him once again, as Rothschild fired him immediately when this information came out, and rightly so, of course.

Another reorganization has taken place, and Warden Anderson has been appointed Regional Administrator of this Region, which is one of five, and consists primarily of SPSM. Don Houseworth is also one of the Regional Administrators, of the Western Region. Bob and I do keep in touch with him and consider him our friend.

I am beginning to keep my eyes open for another line of work! I am wearing an engagement ring on my left hand, and Bob and I would like to marry, now that my divorce is final. Again, the problem may be that although Marvin is my immediate supervisor, we both take orders from Bob, who is the Administrator and in charge of the Psychological Services Unit. Should we marry, this arrangement might not sit well with Civil Service. Actually, Bob is starting to encourage me to leave, for he feels that if serious trouble should erupt, his concern for my safety would complicate the quick decisions he would be called on to make at such a time.

And speaking of "trouble"--- I am really beginning to wonder if I am living on borrowed time, continuing to work here in Seven Block. Security is frighteningly poor now, with the severe overcrowding and so few officers in the block to maintain control. I know I have already had a few close calls, but an incident that happened the other day really got my attention. My involvement started when I was working at my desk with my back to the door, and I heard the door open. In itself, this is not alarming, as residents continue to walk in unannounced from time to time. However, this resident was starting to close the door and had a leer on his face that wasn't difficult to interpret, as he said, "I'm

dialogues #20

Michigan Department of Corrections   July, 1977

| Theodore Koehler | Rudolf H. Stahlberg | Charles E. Anderson | Donald E. Houseworth |

Administrators Named
State Prisons Regionalized

Management of Michigan's prisons changed slightly under a new regionalized organization which began operation July 15.

In the new organization, the state is divided into four regions supervised by administrators under Robert Brown Jr., who heads the department's Bureau of Correctional Facilities.

The regional administrators are expected to help Brown give more personalized attention to the state's expanding prison system. Previously, almost all prison wardens and superintendents reported directly to Brown; now they will report to the administrator in the region to which they are assigned and the administrators will, in turn, report to Brown.

Under the arrangement, Brown is expected to have more time to develop policy and work on planning and budgeting.

"This new structure will allow for much closer supervision and assistance to individual heads of institutions. This is especially crucial as new institutions are added in the coming months and years," Director Johnson said.

The regions and their administrators:

Southeastern Michigan: This region, under the direction of Rudolf H. Stahlberg, covers the state-run Women's Division of the Detroit House of Correction and the Huron Valley Correctional Facility near Ypsilanti, which will replace it late this summer; the new men's maximum security prison nearby; the proposed prison at the Wayne County Child Development Center; the proposed prison in the Hudson's Warehouse in downtown Detroit; the Cassidy Lake Technical School near Chelsea; the proposed minimum security prison in southeastern Michigan; and the Corrections Camp Program, which has headquarters in Grass Lake near Jackson.

Stahlberg, 40, has been supervisor of the department's Special Programs Division, which directs operation of halfway houses and similar community programs throughout the state since 1973. Previously, he headed up probation and parole services in Bay City, and also has

been a parole and probation agent in Lansing, Battle Creek and Wayne County.

Western Michigan: This region, under the the direction of Donald E. Houseworth, Ph.D., contains the proposed prison near Holland, the Muskegon Correctional Facility, the Michigan Training Unit, the Michigan Reformatory and the Riverside Correctional Facility, all in Ionia.

Houseworth, 41, has been assistant deputy director in charge of operations within the Bureau of Correctional Facilities since 1976. Previously, he was in charge of the Psychological Services Unit at the department's Reception and Guidance Center near Jackson.

The State Prison of Southern Michigan at Jackson: This prison complex, which includes the Reception and Guidance Center, the new northside unit and the Trusty Division, will constitute a separate region.

(continued on page 2)

Figure 36 - Houseworth and Anderson are among those appointed Regional Administrators.

in here for rape, you know." I guess I once again reacted mostly from instinct, for instead of trying to get away or use the phone, I rose from my chair and started walking *toward* him, saying, "Is that right? That's interesting!" Apparently this was so unexpected a reaction that the man began retreating backward all the way out the door, and then he disappeared into the crowd of inmates in the block. I called Control, and was told that the officers were next door in Janet's office, as someone had walked in on her and attempted to strangle her. Fortunately, Janet is a large lady and was able to fight off her attacker--- and then I guess he saw that I was convenient as his next target! Janet and I were both fortunate to have come through this, shaken, but all right. However, I believe Janet is seriously considering leaving, now. I had felt that she was uncomfortable working here, ever since she started a few months ago. And maybe now it's getting to be time for me to go, too. More and more women are being hired to work here at SPSM, in various positions, and I do think this is a good thing. But sooner or later, a tragedy is sure to happen that involves one of them. This will always be a dangerous place for anyone to work, but it really is especially hazardous for women, as I'm sure we are seen as weaker and more vulnerable. And where else but in a prison will you find as many predatory sex offenders in one setting?!

Even though safety is always an underlying concern, it seems to be the day to day frustrations with a system that isn't working very well, that tend to eat away at my willingness to commit much more of my life to this job. The genuine attempts by Bob, as PSU Administrator, to improve the conditions and pressures under which we are presently working, are being ignored by the higher-ups. Rothschild attended one of our staff meetings recently, and got an earful on items contributing to the discontent and frustration of staff. The consensus of staff at the conclusion of the meeting (as written in the staff meeting minutes---) "He didn't even *hear* us!"

A short time later, a number of us got together and decided to inform the Superintendent, via the PSU Administrator, of our dissatisfaction in writing. The letter was entitled, "Staff Concerns Regarding Professional Functioning" and contained phrases such as "Staff members are quite angry"--- and "intolerably draining caseload" and "repeated disregard shown to us as professionals." I was happy to be the second person of the eleven who signed---

TO: Robert R. Walsh, Ph.D.
Administrator Psychological Services Unit

DATE: February 1, 1978

FROM: Psychological Services Unit Staff

SUBJECT: Staff Concerns Regarding Professional Functioning

Psychological Services Unit staff members have become
increasingly concerned regarding the non-professional
manner in which we are treated, particularly in reference
to our total lack of input into decisions which affect
optimal performance of our responsibilities as clinicians.
Specifically, we are very distressed regarding current
speculations surrounding the office displacement of our
colleagues on base on well as plans in the near future to
further increase our caseload. Staff members are quite
angry over possible plans to enlarge the infirmary in
7-block at the expense of clinicians. Implementation
of these plans would manifest a callous disregard for the
rights and needs of clinicians. For a professional to
function effectively, basic working condition issues must
be attendend to. We are certainly not asking for newly
furnished offices, carpeting, and air-conditioning, only
bare necessities including; adequate office space,,
adequate lighting, minimal ventilation, and reasonable noise
control. If clinicians are to be employed within the
Reception and Guidance Center, administrative priorities
must be carefully examined and decisions made based upon
the greatest good to the greatest number of individuals.

In another area it should also be realized that we are
processing men through R&GC at maximal efficiency in view
of the tremendous strain and pressure we all work
under. We have on previous occasions been asked to
take extra cases, cancel our group therapy sessions,
and "squeeze" extra trancases into our group psychotherapy
time period. Also, we are frequently asked to process
cases without complete institutional files and without
adequate psychometrics. Many of us have felt the need to
choose to bring some of our work home so as to maintain
high standards of excellence. We are not assembly line
workers and will not function as such. We recognize the
importance of the transcases yet any clinician cannot
justifiably be expected to produce more than six transcases
per eight-hour day. In fact, it is very difficult to do
an adequate job on even six cases, especially with all the
technical non-clinical information we have to provide,
incomplete files, and the additional processing time
required by the new risk screening (without any adjustment
made for this in our caseload). We feel very strongly
about increments in our already intolerably draining caseload
and clinicians cannot handle more than three cases in any
given four hour period. Exceptions to this can be made
for clinicians doing API's, although even in these instances

B

API's should only be scheduled for either the morning or afternoon-not both. Aditionally, we are frequently harassed about recalling cases. We do not have any problems with accountability. However, it must be recognized that recalls for purposes of crisis intervention, duty therapy, consultation on problem cases, need for current psychometric data, and scheduling conflicts are legitimate and valid reasons for not processing all transcases assigned that day. Our ability to effectively assess and conceputalize a man psychodynamically is seriously impaired under conditions in which we are exploited and we cannot tolerate such conditions. Also, the time a clinican has surrounding a group therapy session is utilized for the preparation of parole board, progress, termination, and related psychological reports. This time is also consumed in writing therapy notes, continued therapeutic intervention with group members, consultion with staff members, as well as to explore one's own feelings relative to the therapy session and related matters. Cases should not be scheduled during these time periods except in emergency situations.

In conclusion, it is hoped that this memo will shed some insight into the dissatisfaction, frustration, and anger we feel over the repeated disregard shown to us not only as professionals but also as individuals. We see ourselves as capable, responsible, intelligent and dedicated to our clients. We can most effectively be utilized when concern and action is taken in regards to our needs and capabilities. We have much to offer yet can only function optimally in a responsive and concerned environment.

cc: Supt.
    Dr.
    Dr.
    File

SIGNED BY ALL P.S.U. STAFF

Figure 37 - Previous page and above — I was the second to sign this staff protest which went to the Superintendent via the PSU Administrator

**MICHIGAN
DEPARTMENT
of
CORRECTIONS**

TO: _____, Ph.D., Superintendent
Reception and Guidance Center

DATE: April 19, 1978

FROM: _____, M.A., Clinical Psychologist
Psychological Services Unit

SUBJECT: Superintendent-Representative Meeting Agenda Items

1. The Psychological Services Unit Staff is having a good deal of difficulty with handling the crisis intervention requests. We are requesting that when a staff member refers a crisis to a clinician, that a reason also be sent. Sometimes we don't know why we are seeing a particular individual and that individual does not always communicate.

2. The scheduling of Parole Board evaluations, reduced custody screenings and discharge summaries for Trusty Division is hampered considerably by the lack of office space. What can be done about this problem?

3. The scheduling of psych calls on the staggered system is not working. The men are not being let out of their cells and there is consequently much wasted time. Can we go back to the previous system of having all persons released from their cells at the same time?

4. There are complaints that several men have stated that the MMPI tape is of poor quality, especially toward the end. Can this be checked and corrected?

5. There is significant support for custody and treatment learning each others' jobs. Comments about "bankers hours" when coming in at 10 o'clock after a particularly heavy group session are hard to take even if it is meant jokingly. The PSU staff knows that this problem can go in the other direction also and would like to work it out before more significant problems arise. When can the program be implemented?

6. There have been many typing errors that change the entire meaning of a sentence; i.e. ("raped by his mother" instead of "raised by his mother".) Having them retyped holds up the reports and also puts extra work on the typists. We in the psych unit will certainly try to talk more clearly; can the typists be a little more careful in regard to their finished product?

7. Is there any way that we can get the pressure sensitive element in the risk screening sheets? This was asked for and promised to us in December by Deputy Director _____, but nothing has happened thus far. *BACK ORDERED BY PRINTS*

8. Has anyone informed Mr. _____ of the length of time it takes to fill out the risk screening sheets? For some reason, it was apparently stated to him there was no particular problem.

9. The clock in the bubble is 5 minutes faster than the one inside and from the correct time. Consequently when we leave, the bubble is already closed early and are forced to leave through 6-Block. Can the clock be corrected?

10. The files in GOS are still being held out too long by various individuals throughout the institution. This interrupts the continuity of Parole Board evaluations. Can something be done?

Figure 38 - Above and following page – Multiple problems continue in 1978 – note circled items 5 & 12.

11. The trailer offices are missing the handles on the windows. We have attempted to get replacements, but to no avail. Can something be accomplished at higher levels?

12. The therapy room is still extremely poor. The one in the old CSU, that was meant as a replacement for the subhall room, is dark and the windows are broken out, so that on cold days it is not at all conducive to appropriate therapeutic situations. When are we going to be allowed to have reasonable facilities for conducting something is supposedly important to the Department's functioning.

13. There is still much concern an anger about being forced to do transcases without PSI's or incomplete information relevant to the case.

14. The Bender Gestalt is being administered backwards. Several complaints have been made, so can better control on all testing procedures be instituted to insure more reliable information?

15. There is much concern and resentment about the new proposed processing system and the ethically questionably use of the MMPI. Why are we saddled with this system and forced to see that it functions well, without having had any input into its structure?

16. There is still some major concern about inmates handling the psych files, which is viewed by some of the Psychological Services Unit Staff as a breach of confidentiality. Has this ever been investigated and can it be tightened up?

17. There is a problem with having enough of Page 1 of the Transcase Sheets, 104A. This forces recalls and delays, so can something be done about the ordering process so that we do not run out quite so often?

18. We are having a lot of trouble with referring psychotics to the Clinic. They are kicked back because of a lack of bed space and the Psychological Services Unit clinicians are having to spend excessive amounts of time following up the entire problem.

GR/dmc

But of course, nothing has changed. The answer is always the same, "Just be patient and wait until PSU is finally moved out of Seven Block and into Top Six, after Clinical Services leaves, and things will be better." Of course, things always have been better for CSU, housed in Top Six where there are windows, and better security, and rest rooms--- and even drinkable coffee! At times, the planned move seems like "pie in the sky!" And in the meantime, Rothschild and/or Lansing office keep making changes that affect us and our workload, but without any input from us, of course. All the time that was saved from the implementation of my Transcase checklist has been taken up by a new "risk screening" that Lansing

Office requires us to complete on each man we interview. None of us are against the screening, it's just that if we see six men a day and the screening takes an extra ten minutes per man, where is that hour supposed to come from? Many of us do take work home now, in order to catch up. There are thousands of men currently on the waiting list for therapy, and the counties sometimes send busloads of 50 to 80 new arrivals to Seven Block in a day. No one can keep up. Recently, we heard that because the typists were so far behind in their work, someone farther up the chain ordered a large quantity of the tapes that contain our intake clinical reports, destroyed before being typed!! And the latest idea, which really upsets me, is that the department plans to get rid of all the files on residents' previous incarcerations that are older than a certain date. I believe that if this is done, it will greatly handicap us in trying to put together a coherent picture of the events throughout an individual's life that eventually led up to his current offense, and his present mental status. Obviously, the information we get from the man himself when he is interviewed, is sometimes far from accurate!

But I must get on with other things that have been happening. Connie is now working part time, but for the Program Bureau in Lansing, so that she can continue her treatments there. Bob and I received a wonderful gift from her recently, a little black kitten that Bob has named Vulcan. We enjoy him so much, and he will continue to remind us of her friendship.

An item in "The Spectator" (the inmate newspaper) has really upset me. It seems that the older man who exposed himself to me in Earl Grier' office that day, recently tried to hang himself in Five West. If he has been locked in that hellhole all this time, I can understand the suicide attempt, whether it was real or a "cry for help." I never did feel that he was a real threat to me or anyone else. His questionable mental status no doubt led to his inappropriate behavior in my presence. This man, like Levon, was *punished* when he should have been *treated!* Perhaps I should have followed up at the time--- now I wish that I had. At any rate, at last he has been removed from Five Block and is now residing in Top Six, where he should have been taken in the first place!

I do want to mention briefly a few of the participants I encountered in my therapy groups this year. Of course, all of the men become interesting, one way or another, as you get to know them. It is rare that I take such a dislike to one man that I cannot overcome my feelings as time goes on, but it happened with

Terry. This man is not just a pedophile, but was earning his living by photographing children being exploited for sex--- and quite successfully for him, too. I gather that his productions not only had a large audience, but that he had affiliations with many others in the same business. The file even told of his physical abuse of his own small children! Terry, however, denied this, and felt that because of his involvement with others in the same business, his assistance to the police in arresting and prosecuting his business partners was invaluable and should have been rewarded. He said he was dismayed when he himself was also sent to prison, after he had been such a help to the authorities! As I mentioned before, pedophiles are heartily detested by the majority of inmates in prison, and probably because of that, Terry, in his insecurity, would usually try to occupy the chair immediately beside me, as though appealing to me for protection. I never was able to overcome the revulsion I felt for this man.

Other pedophiles I encountered in my groups did not bring about the reaction I had to Terry. One elderly man in my group had been a pastor of a church. Unfortunately, he also had a sexual obsession for young girls. And it was an obsession that was so overpowering, it had landed him in prison several times. He seemed a very pathetic case to me, as he admitted both his actions and the fact that he probably would revert to that behavior, should he ever be paroled.

I had two men, in different groups, who had been prosecuted for having sex with their teen-age daughters. One was unrepentant, because, "She came onto me!" The other was so ashamed that he could not face the group to talk about it, and suddenly one day, got up and left the room. Since this is an offense for "skating" (not being where you are supposed to be), I left the group very briefly in order to find him, standing in the hallway with a look of grief on his face that I will not soon forget.

I mentioned Bernard before, the man whose wife was to undergo brain surgery. Unfortunately, she died, and I will always remember him as he told me, "I'll never be able to kiss her again---

Spring, 1978

Figure 39 - Dr. & Mrs. Robert Walsh, April, 1978.

I will be leaving soon. Bob and I are going to be married April 21st and my last day on the job will be about a week later (plus a week then that I have left of vacation time.) I have such mixed emotions about my work here, even now, though I have had quite a long time to mull over the pros and cons. I feel very frustrated and angry that those of us doing the mandated work with inmates, are so consistently denied input into decisions that directly affect what we do. I deplore the working conditions we have to put up with daily. I hope that someday, some way, there will be less acrimony between custody and treatment. More recognition should be given to the part psychologists can play in rehabilitation, given half a chance. Some see us as an impediment to the good order of the institution, while others expect us to perform miracles in our once-a-week therapy groups, conducted under such anti-therapeutic conditions! And for me, so much remains unfinished. I feel badly about leaving my groups, even though I still feel I was not as much help to my therapy men as I would have liked to be. I will miss my fellow therapists, although with Bob the Administrator here, I will no doubt be able to hear about them frequently. There is also the possibility that Bob and I might set up a private practice in the community with several of the others on the staff, with me taking over the day shift! I will also hate to say goodbye to Cowboy and the cadre, who have so diligently provided me with protection for so long. I wish them well and will tell them so, and thank them very much!

But now, with only days left for me to work here, I would like to report on one pleasant event, and of one encounter that really shook my self-confidence recently. The pleasant event came about because my therapy group member, Benny, really wanted me to meet his wife. Normally, this would have been very hard to bring about, but it just happened that the prison branch of the Jaycees had their yearly banquet coming up. At this event, inmate members' wives are allowed to attend with them, inside Trusty Division, which makes it a very special occasion indeed. Another inmate I had been receiving epistles (kites) from, over the two years since I had interviewed him in Seven Block, sent me a very elegantly worded invitation also, from his position as the "Public Relations Director" of the "Jacktown" S. C. Jaycees! So how could I refuse?? It was an evening meeting, and I attended somewhat warily, all by myself. It was a large gathering with a number of speakers, and of course, many inmates and their guests, and I felt quite honored to have been invited. And yes, I did meet Benny's wife and liked her. I do hope she will continue to stand by him when he is paroled and that her love will help him finally overcome his compulsions--- yes, I do hope so!

It is hard for me not to have high hopes for group members I have become acquainted with, and met with, and yes, even cared about, over a long period of time. But the second memorable event that happened this spring really shook my self-confidence in my efforts as a therapist. I was in the bubble one morning, about to pass by the bullpen, which was really crammed with new arrivals. I make it a point not to direct my attention there, just as I never gaze into cells in Seven Block as I walk by, for I respect the men's need for some little bit of privacy. But this once, I did glance up just as one man put his head down and tried to turn away--- and I recognized Joe, the man who had been paroled after a board member had called me for my opinion. I stammered inanely, "Joe, what happened?" (as if he could tell me, there!) and he mumbled something about "messing up." Later, I learned from the staff member who did his intake interview, that Joe had requested not to be assigned to me while in Seven Block, because he was so ashamed. Yes, he had "messed up," all right, and had sexually assaulted a child in his own family! This brought me to a really low point. What had made me think that I could do anything to change the lives of convicted felons? Over the past two and a half years, I have been questioning my skills as a therapist for men in prison. What am I doing here, anyway? How can I understand the lives of men sent here, so full of experiences I have been spared--- Many files have told of unloving or abusive or absent parents, how can I know what that is like? The veterans returning from an unappreciated war--- I've never had their horrific experiences! And the mentally ill, like Levon, who I'm unable to help in spite of good intentions--- Should I have ever come here? Did my presence in the prison make any difference??

At any rate, I have made my decision to leave. Maybe I will go on to counsel women who have reached crises in their lives. I've been there. And I recall that this was my original intention, when I felt I wanted to become a psychologist. It seems so long ago. Working in an all-male prison has certainly been the experience of a lifetime for me, and I will never get the sound of the buzzers or the clanging of the cell doors out of my mind, I am sure. I think that I have grown, as a result of working here. I have made friends, and enemies, and unexpectedly, I turned my personal life upside down also! I am less dependent and more assertive than when I first entered Seven Block. And I am also less fearful, which may or may not be a good thing, in a place like this. (I learned early on that it was best never to look or carry myself in here as though I was afraid!) I feel good about some accomplishments, like coming up with the idea of a checklist "transcase," and then developing it. And I think I led the way for more women to work with men who are in prison, whether in positions as psychologists, or officers or maybe someday, in the higher-up hierarchy of the Department of Corrections.

mentally ill
therapy room

RECEPTION AND GUIDANCE CENTER SUPERINTENDENT-UNIT HEAD MEETING

April 27, 1978

Present: ____, ____, Robert Walsh, ____, and

The minutes of the Wardens' and Superintendents' Meeting were read and reviewed.

Mr. ____ brought up the subject of the shortage of R&GC Cadre. In particular, Mr. ____ emphasized with our yard program we had to hire a yardman. Lt. ____ was given the assignment to find an appropriate Cadreman to serve as yard man.

Mr. ____ brought up the subject of individuals processing through the Reception and Guidance Center where the files had been "lost". The files referred to were the files from an individual's previous incarceration. We have made a decision to wait one month's time and if the file did not appear, we would write Lansing and ask them to formulate a duplicate copy for our purposes.

Dr. Walsh brought up the subject of the great number of mentally ill individuals in the State Prison of Southern Michigan. Dr. Walsh emphasized that it was in his staff's opinion that a protective environment would have to be formulated for these individuals. He reviewed in detail the large number of psychotics who are under treatment in detention and/or 6-Block. He emphasized that the large number of crisis interventions now occurring in the State Prison of Southern Michigan was cutting into the transcase processing of the Reception and Guidance Center. He emphasized that a record number of crisis interventions have occurred during the past month. Most of these crisis interventions entailed mentally ill individuals acting out.

Dr. Walsh also discussed in detail his difficulties in securing group therapy rooms. The room formerly used by the Psychological Services Unit staff to conduct group psychotherapy in the State Prison of Southern Michigan has been taken over by the Office of Substance Abuse. At the present time the staff is using a group room on what was formerly known at Top-6. This room, however, is lacking windows and does not have any electricity. Dr. Walsh is concerned that when the renovation of Top-6 might start that this therapy room will be taken from the Psychological Services Unit. He further emphasized that this problem has also manifested in Trusty Division. The group psychotherapists in Trusty Divison do not have a permanent room and are displaced for many programs. The most recent being a min-ister administering some type of tests to five individuals. This forced a therapist to cancel a scheduled therapy session. Dr. Walsh emphasized that the securing of new Psychologists for the purpose of treatment as well as the advant of Transcase Processors will be to no avail if some type of permanent room arrangement cannot be arranged. Dr. Walsh reports it appears to him and his staff that members of the State Prison of Southern Michigan do not place great emphasis on the value of psycho-therapy and his staff feel somewhat in a bind. They feel that the Parole Board and other individuals place some importance on therapy but he is not receiving the supportive assistance necessary, namely rooms to conduct the said therapy. Superintendent ____ informed Dr. Walsh that he will pursue this matter with Regional Administrator Anderson. When Superintendent ____ inquired into the usage of rooms in the various cell blocks, Dr. Walsh reported that this is of only

Figure 40 - Above and following page — Bob reports on psychotics in detention, and my last therapy group meeting in Trusty!

193

limited value. He emphasized that group rooms in cell blocks are effective for violent or acting out classifications of group psychotherapy. However, he has found from his experience it is not effective for sexual offenders as they will not open up for fear that their pathology will get out in the cell block. It also has been Dr. Walsh's experience that if a therapist is making in-roads in psychotherapy that residents have a tendency to go to the resident unit manager and request a transfer out of the block to avoid the therapist. It is his opinion that rooms in the cell blocks can be utilized but only for a limited number of groups. Superintendent   informed Dr. Walsh to explore the possibility of varied work schedules for the Psychologist so that perhaps we could work into the room schedules in the school systems after their normal working hours.

Lt.   reported that he is experiencing no difficulties with the custodial complement and they had no concerns or issues.

Captain   reported that the riot training is under way and that the officers are participating wholeheartedly.

Superintendent   discussed the progress of the plans for splitting off the youthful offender processing from the older offenders.

Respectfully submitted,

                              , Ph.D., Superintendent

JP/dmc

Finale

My last working day at the prison has come and gone. I have locked my office door for the last time, entered and climbed the ramp and heard the doors slam shut behind me. I guess it would have been nice to have heard a fanfare, a drumroll, something to make my exit significant, but other than a few goodbyes and well-wishes and handshakes on the way out, my exit, like most of the day, was pretty ordinary. The celebrating was done a week ago, at our wedding party, so there really was not much left to be said. Except to my group members yesterday, of course, and even that last meeting will be a bittersweet memory. For some time, now, the radio room has no longer been available for use by the therapists, and most recently, I have been meeting with my original group in a room over in Trusty Division. But yesterday, of all days, that room was not available, and we were finally forced to use the only space left, which was in one corner of the busy waiting room! There was no privacy, of course, and little time left when we were finally all assembled there. Worse, there was no real chance for anyone to express themselves, at this, our final meeting!

So I am leaving today both angry and sad, for I see that last group meeting as one last example of how little the psychologists' work here is valued! I know full well how hard Bob is working to improve things, but there is a limit to what he can accomplish. I am thinking of writing a letter--- maybe to Don Houseworth, who hired me, and who now has a high position in the department. It may not make a bit of difference in the long run, but hey, getting it all out will (maybe) make *me* feel better!

Letter to Don Houseworth

May 2, 1978

Dear Don,

I'm writing to let you know that I am resigning my position at the end of this week. I felt that I wanted to let you know this and my reasons for leaving, since you originally gambled on hiring me as the first female psychologist in the reception center.

I hope you can remember the enthusiasm I felt for my work during the initial months with the Unit! If you can, then you'll have some idea of the anger and bitterness I now feel as I cut my career with the department short. Although I'm sure some staff members in the past have used their work experience at the prison as a steppingstone to a "better" position elsewhere, this wasn't my intention, as you know. In fact, I became resigned to the pretty intolerable conditions in order to do work I saw as rewarding. I coped with the dirty, stuffy office, the parade of cockroaches across my desk, the incessant noise, the lack of a lounge or ladies room. I agreed that coffee breaks were out of the question. Like most of the staff, I took work home again and again because I was never allowed quite enough time to do what I considered an acceptable job. Through all of this, I kept going because I sincerely believed that what I was doing had some meaning. I saw myself doing my part to aid an overtaxed and beleaguered system that was enlightened and basically treatment oriented. I tried to transmit my enthusiasm to new staff members after I was placed in charge of their initial two week training. My philosophy was that if all of us really worked hard, our efforts would bear fruit and some of the badly needed changes would come about. If you recall, I mentioned to you before you left, my idea of saving psychologists' time on evaluations by instigating a transcase checklist. I was encouraged that this suggestion was accepted, and that I was able to be involved in its design and in initiating its use. This and a number of other special projects sustained my belief that the department was progressive and even responsive when possible.

Unfortunately, events this past year have steadily eroded my faith that we are working in a progressive system, particularly as regards treatment. I no longer find credible the excuse that population pressures alone are responsible for retarding or preventing necessary changes. I am especially upset by the negative attitude throughout the department toward psychologists and their role in the system. We have to contend daily with the obvious disregard for our treatment efforts. The constant struggle just to have access to adequate space in which to do group therapy, is frustrating and time consuming. Since I've been employed at Jackson Prison, I've had to cope with doing groups in that ugly, unsuitable room off the subhall, with broken windows, excessive heat or cold, garbage trucks being emptied just outside, acoustics and noise so bad that I missed about a third of what was said. (Now that that room has arbitrarily been taken away from us for use by the substance abuse program, we find it is being completely renovated with paneling and other amenities.) After I moved my group to a vacant room at the Clinical Services Unit last fall, I found my men detained week after week from getting in for one technicality or another, to the obvious delight of those manning the gate. I finally gave up and moved to the Visitor's Center at Trusty Division. There I found that the rooms are doled out on a first come, first served basis. Just this past week, I found the large room I have been using regularly at the same time, pre-empted by a minister with five men. He very rudely refused when asked if he and his group would mind moving to a small room that was available; the people at the desk disclaimed responsibility, and an appeal to the Deputy Warden was to no avail. My last opportunity to meet with my nine men took place in a corner of the visiting room, non-private and twenty minutes late starting. It would seem that the group therapy program is a "paper program" included only to impress outsiders, because it certainly isn't given even half a chance to succeed. It may be that there is a lack of understanding of how emotionally draining it is to conduct groups even under the best of conditions. The need for privacy is also apparently not recognized, as I've had as many as three interruptions for "count" during one session, when I had already posted the list on the door as instructed!

It has been frustrating, too, to see the time saving effected by the checklist transcase completely eaten up by the extra work of filling out multiple sheets for statistical risk prediction. The lack of enthusiasm for doing transcases stems largely from the lack of time allotted to do an adequate job. So it is discouraging to have to cut minutes off vital interview time in order to struggle with messy carbon paper and numerous forms. But time is an important commodity, and we never have enough. We are held responsible for familiarizing ourselves with the contents of a three inch thick file in the same time that we are given to peruse files containing reports so scanty that we are forced to rely almost entirely on the resident's story. We find that old files are being destroyed despite our protests and without regard for the information they contain. We write tickets on men who are not on the benches when called, only to find out later that they weren't unlocked by custody--- who tear up our tickets. "Recalls" for any reason are anathema, because it seems that ultimately, the psychologists are blamed for any breakdown in the production-line processing of men through the Reception Center. It seems to slip everyone's attention that our staff members have multiple duties and that the complexity of the work is increasing daily. The manual I compiled for staff training a year and a half ago contained 250 pages. The revision completed today contains 369 pages. Training itself, which was very brief and haphazard when I began, now is barely completed in two weeks. This makes a large staff turnover particularly unprofitable for the department. It is also unnecessary. The majority of the psychologists at present are hard-working, responsible, professionally competent people who care enough about what they are doing to put up with the shoddy offices and hazardous conditions. I trained most of them and feel that I know them well. I know that most take work home to complete on their own time. All of us experience the emotional fatigue at the end of each day from having to struggle with the often overwhelming problems of our population without the time to recoup through "breaks" or even consultation with other staff. But by and large, it is not the work itself or even the setting that drives competent people to look for work elsewhere. It is that intangible but all-pervasive departmental attitude I mentioned before.

The disregard for the Psychological Services Unit has been under-scored by the imposition of the latest scheme for a "reorganization of the Reception Center." It is difficult to believe that changes with far-reaching consequences have been ordered without benefit of input from those whose work is most affected. It seems unthinkable that with the need for therapy so well documented, (with several thousand on the waiting list) the plan is to replace a number of psychologists with counselor-aides. That no one in the Psychological Services Unit was informed of the proposal for our restructuring prior to the submission of the plan to the Regional Administrator, is reprehensible! When the substance of the proposal was given to us by the Warden, a number of us were concerned enough to spend our time evenings and several weekends doing a detailed and hopefully unbiased assessment of the impact of these changes. We also similarly evaluated several other alternatives that were suggested by our staff. But our efforts appear to have been wasted, for to our knowledge, no one in Lansing office made even a pretense of interest in the consequences of their decision on processing efficiency, effective use of psychologists' time, or ultimately, the best interests of the residents. I cannot believe that in the long run, anything will be gained by the planned degrading of services. At this point, I am feeling that the impact of the checklist transcase in making such changes possible, will have been negative rather than positive, when roughly 50% of the men will not be evaluated by a psychologist. Such rule by fiat, from the point of view of those carrying it out, does not elicit a spirit of cooperation, particularly when the basis for the decision is unknown.

Additionally, many of us do experience difficulty, in varying degrees, with the ethical considerations connected with extracting sensitive and personal information from men who are coerced into therapy with no guarantees of confidentiality,...

I do have mixed emotions about leaving, even now. I regret abandoning my therapy groups, as I am quite convinced that a female therapist in sex offender groups is a definite asset if not indispensable! I'll miss the heavy traffic through my office door of men who come because they've heard the "lady psych" will at least listen to their problems. And I'll especially miss my colleagues on the staff, who are a wonderful group of people, and my friends. But at this point, the negatives outweigh the positives and my efforts to extract some sense of meaning from my work have been overwhelmed by feelings of futility, even anger. This is my protest. I hope this letter will help you understand my decision.

Sincerely,

Jean

After Words 2013

Shortly after writing what I had believed was the final word in "There's a *Woman* in Here!" I realized that interested readers might legitimately feel that the story wasn't concluded to their satisfaction. After all, it is now 2013, and many years have passed since 1978! With that in mind, I am once again taking pen in hand (a figure of speech only, as I am once again sitting at my computer) and will give a brief account of happenings since I left work in Seven Block, both in my life and in the lives of some of the others I spoke of in the book.

As I mentioned in the Prologue, I did return to the Psychological Services Unit for a while in 1981, filling in for a staff member who was off work on medical leave. In order to avoid conflict over being supervised by my husband, still the Administrator of Psychological Services, Adam Rothschild volunteered to oversee my work, and wrote me a letter welcoming me back. However, this was mostly a paper arrangement, and I seldom had any direct contact with him that spring. By then, the Psychological Services Unit was no longer located in Seven Block, but had taken over the Top Six quarters vacated by the Clinical Services Unit, who had been moved elsewhere in the state. Working out of Top Six was very different. I actually had an office with a window, and there was a ladies room nearby (at last!) as there were now a number of women that Bob had hired as psychologists since I left in 1978. He had increased the staff a great deal, hiring people of either sex, and any race or sexual identity, as long as they were competent to do the job.

Very little that happened during that five and a half months of half day employment stands out in my mind, except that it was quite difficult trying to fill the shoes of another therapist, and I faced considerable resentment from some of her therapy group members. By then Seven Block cadre, if not disbanded, were no longer seen, and I had no further contact with our former clerks or Cowboy and his crew. I did not find it difficult to walk away once more, when the time came. If I had been there exactly one month longer, I would have been able to write of my memories of Jackson Prison's worst riot since the devastating one in the 1950's. Bob and all the PSU staff survived unharmed but shaken, of course. Although I was at home at that time, I was seldom far from ongoing news reports because of concern about Bob and the others inside. Somehow, though, it became more personal to me, when I saw a picture in the newspaper of the remains of the OD. The Rose Room had been destroyed by the inmates, who evidently had vented their fury on this favorite gathering place of prison employees. Somehow, this finalized in my mind that from now on, my connection with the prison would be through hearing of events there from my husband. And Bob did keep me up to date, throughout the remainder of his twenty-five years of work for the Department of Corrections.

My dear friend Connie died of the bone cancer in 1980. She asked someone to call us, to ask us to come to Lansing quickly to visit her, and we were with her the evening before her death. She was at home with her family and seemed at peace, knowing her little boy would be well cared for. As we were getting ready to leave, this fragile, emaciated little person, almost unrecognizable now except for her smile, somehow managed to slide off her hospital bed and walked into the living room to say one last goodbye. That is when I couldn't hold back the tears. I cried all the way back to Jackson that night. Later we heard that our good-looking cadre member, Mark, had fallen in love with Connie and had tried desperately to call her that night. He was denied permission to make that call until the next morning, when it was too late.

Of the three men who first interviewed me when I applied for the position of psychologist with the D.O.C., we have remained most closely in touch with Don Houseworth. He was the Administrator of Psychology when I was hired, and before my departure, he had become Regional Administrator of the Western Region. He retired a number of years ago and moved to Arizona, although he frequently returns to Michigan in the summer. He once took us sailing on Lake Michigan, and graciously forgave me when we had to return to port due to my sudden case of "mal de mer"!

Warden Anderson, though retired from the Department, continues to be a prominent figure in the Jackson area. We have seen him various times over the years, and each time, it is as though we are reconnecting with an old and trusted friend. He was a very positive influence while with the Department of Corrections and we were sorry to see him leave.

This is the former officers' dining room of Southern Michigan Prison. During Friday's prison disturbance, the dining room was set afire. It is built of cement blocks with few windows. The walls held in the heat, baking the interior like an oven. (Citizen Patriot photos by Elaine Thompson)

Figure 41 - The Officers' Dining Room, the Rose Room, was destroyed during the 1981 riot.

Most of the others who worked in Seven Block when I was there moved on, or moved up, and/or are retired by now. Steve Ribby and Earl Grier moved up the ladder and became wardens. Adam Rothschild also became a warden, in Ionia. He graciously invited us both to tour his facility in the late 80's, and then we were treated to dinner with Adam and his new wife. It seemed an unusual reunion indeed! Ronald Halstead left the D.O.C. to take a position in the private sector, as did Edward Benjamin. Jimmy also found a new career as a paralegal. Janet did not remain long after the attack, but of course, more women were hired as psychologists very soon. The rest of the crew I worked with slipped out of our lives eventually. It does seem that many of the clinical staff become disillusioned with work in corrections before very long, just as I had.

I've only been able to follow up on a few of the inmates I dealt with while working in the prison, most of them members of my therapy groups. Sadly, my high, if unrealistic, hopes for Benny were dashed when I learned that he was paroled and then returned to prison for a new offense, this time with a life sentence. I try to balance this awful failure with thoughts of Chet, who was paroled in spite of a life sentence, and who has remained free since his release. Another success story was Daniel. I already mentioned that he married after he was paroled, but I can also add that he actually made the news in a positive way a bit later. It seems that he heard a woman's cries for help one night, and in spite of the possibility that he might somehow be implicated because of his record if he responded, he did intervene and prevented a sexual attack! I console myself with the few successes that I know about. I tried very hard to help my group men, using the skills that I had, though I often felt inadequate for the task. I do feel sure they knew that I cared, however, and sometimes I think that that knowledge alone is therapeutic for some.

Oh yes, of course I must also report that Greg, who stormed out of my group session, apparently did manage to parole. However, he must have been returned with a new sentence, because some years later, I saw his picture in the newspaper, with the account telling of a prisoner who had tossed his hat in the ring and was audaciously making a run for governor. The article also reported that he actually felt that he, an inmate, had a chance to win! I will refrain from commenting except to bow to the good judgment of Michigan voters!

The last time I spoke to Levon, I was working at my desk in Seven Block and received a phone call from George Bowman in Top Six. Apparently someone had *finally* recognized that Levon needed help, and had appropriately referred him to the Clinical Services Unit. George put Levon on the phone to talk with me, but the conversation was very guarded, as I knew George was listening and I didn't know anything of Levon's current mental state. All I could find words for was an assurance to Levon that I had not forgotten him and that I cared about what happened to him. Then in 1977, I received two kites from him from Marquette Prison in the Upper Peninsula. The first was very inappropriate, disturbed, and erotic in content, but the second, written the following day, began by saying, "My dear Jean, I wish I had the power to grant you a dream come true for each and every unpleasant moment I've caused since our friendship began," and ended with the question, "Will you ever forgive me?" On the form where the Department asks the writer to declare the relationship of the recipient, Levon had written "friend." Somehow, that one word touches me, even now. Although I learned the Department's cardinal rule that an employee should *never* become a friend of an inmate, I'm afraid I have trouble understanding the difference between friendship and caring about what happens to someone. Even now, I often wish that I could have done more to help Levon.

On a more positive note, I learned only recently that Cowboy was finally able to break his established pattern of "doing life on the instalment plan". I am so pleased to hear this! Good for you, Cowboy. You and the cadre made me feel so much safer in Seven Block, all those many years ago!

One Corrections Department employee whose life and work I have been able to follow since I left so long ago is, of course, that of my husband, Bob Walsh. After our marriage in 1978, he continued as Administrator of Psychology, at first with responsibility for Psychological Services at the Reception Center in Jackson, and at one time, for D.O.C. psychologists state-wide. He retired in 1999 after 25 gruelling years of work for the Department, during which he did his utmost to strengthen the role of treatment in the prisons. He hired the most capable staff he could find, dealt firmly with the racism inherent in the system, and made many necessary changes. For years, he had many successes and built the Psychological Services unit from a staff of 13 when I left in 1978, to 40 who answered to him before he left. Unfortunately, changes in top personnel in the

Department coincided with a harder view toward the role of incarceration, in the aftermath of several riots. Eventually, Bob's efforts for more humane treatment of prisoners and racial equality for staff brought him into serious conflict with top Department of Corrections management. However, I will not attempt to tell here of the punishing changes in his status and the personal toll that was inflicted, as he stubbornly refused to compromise his values. Those who are interested will soon be able to read his own account of his twenty-five eventful years with the Department of Corrections.

Even though my work in Corrections ended so many years ago, I have never let go of my interest in Jackson Prison and prison work. Because I had been employed there, I was able to understand, as Bob would tell me of his progress and concerns throughout the years he worked as Administrator of Psychology at SPSM. He tells me that the ability to talk with me about events at the Psychological Services Unit at the end of each day was a stress-reliever that few prison workers have, for most say they feel that their spouses could not comprehend what it is really like to work "inside." Bob and I have truly been partners throughout our 35 years of marriage thus far. Of course I still often wonder what our lives would have been like if I had continued as a prison psychologist. As it was, though, until Bob retired, I was at his side whenever allowed or appropriate, whether it was to listen when he testified in court or to the legislature, or to attend meetings with him, or simply to read what he wrote and make suggestions. We both joined the NAACP when the conflict with the Department on racial issues became heated, and enjoyed the friendships we made there. Perhaps my behind-the-scenes support of Bob's efforts to improve conditions did more good than I would have accomplished if I had continued working inside.

I have also pursued many interests other than Corrections since 1978. I have good relationships with my three children, and try to keep up on the accomplishments of four grandchildren and now four great-grandchildren. My greatest loss occurred when my youngest son was killed in an accident while still in his twenties, and that hurt is always with me. I have tried many endeavors. For a while I owned an antique store, which proved to be time consuming but far from rewarding monetarily! I was also a partner in a private practice of psychology with Bob and several others from the staff at the prison, with me making up the day shift. It was interesting that one of my first clients was a female guard from the prison, who was suffering greatly from the antagonism of male custody staff. I have followed my interest in architecture through planning and then helping to build several houses, including the one Bob and I now live in. I also enjoy building and decorating scale model houses, some complete with electric lights and one with a working fountain in the yard! I inherited my talented son's camera after his death and have won awards for some of my photographs. I also renewed my interest in art and recently exhibited 27 of my paintings. But my life's most important work, I believe, was done in those years working inside what was then the world's largest walled prison. I don't know if what I did there was of any great importance. But I do think that I was somehow led there by my belief that I could develop and use my talents for a worthwhile purpose, a belief engendered so long ago at a weekend camp meeting. I would like to think that just maybe, my work in the prison had a lasting impact in some way that I might never know, or even imagine.